1978

DUKE UNIVERSITY PUBLICATIONS

MELVILLE'S RELIGIOUS THOUGHT

MELVILLE'S RELIGIOUS THOUGHT

An Essay in Interpretation

by

WILLIAM BRASWELL

OCTAGON BOOKS

A DIVISION OF FARRAR, STRAUS AND GIROUX

New York   1977

Reprinted 1973
by special arrangement with the Duke University Press
Second Octagon printing 1977

OCTAGON BOOKS
A DIVISION OF FARRAR, STRAUS & GIROUX, INC.
19 Union Square West
New York, N.Y. 10003

Library of Congress Cataloging in Publication Data

Braswell, William, 1907-
    Melville's religious thought.

    Original ed. issued in series: Duke University publications.
    Includes bibliographical references.
    1. Melville, Herman, 1819-1891—Religion and ethics.   I. Title.
[PS2388.R4B7   1973]   813.3   73-324
ISBN 0-374-90945-8

Manufactured by Braun-Brumfield, Inc.
Ann Arbor, Michigan
Printed in the United States of America

TO THE MEMORY

OF

My Father and Mother

FOREWORD

SINCE the first chapter of this book contains most of what might be said by way of introduction to the more specific essays that follow, I cheerfully forego the gesture of making additional prefatory remarks in this place.

I cannot, however, deny myself the pleasure of expressing here my gratitude to the friends and scholarly acquaintances who have helped me in the development of my study, though they are in no sense to be held responsible for any errors in interpretation or flaws in style that may appear. To Mrs. Eleanor Melville Metcalf I am indebted for valuable information, as well as for the privilege of examining some of the annotated and marked volumes that were formerly in Herman Melville's library. For courtesies and assistance of various kinds I am obligated to Raymond M. Weaver, of Columbia University; Victor H. Paltsits, formerly of the New York Public Library; John H. Birss, of Rutgers University; and the late Robert S. Forsythe. The manuscript was read by Napier Wilt, of the University of Chicago; Henry A. Murray, of Harvard University; Willard Thorp, of Princeton University; H. L. Creek, of Purdue University; Merton M. Sealts, formerly of the University of Missouri; and Walter Bezanson, of Dartmouth College. For their stimulating criticism I am deeply grateful.

But my greatest indebtedness is to my good friend Kendall B. Taft, of Central College in Chicago. When I went into naval service he took over my manuscript, prepared the final copy, and submitted it to the publishers. He labored over the form of documentary notes, he drew up the index, he read the proof. In short, the book would not now be published but for his efforts and sacrifices. For such generous aid I can offer no adequate thanks.

April 15, 1943.   W. B.

CONTENTS

MELVILLE'S RELIGIOUS THOUGHT

CHAPTER I

RELIGIOUS BACKGROUND AND INFLUENCES

ON HIS WAY to the Holy Land in 1856, Herman Melville stopped to visit his old friend and former neighbor Hawthorne, now consul at Liverpool. One day out among the sand dunes near Southport they had a long conversation. Melville briefly referred to it in his journal as "Good talk."[1] Hawthorne wrote in his journal:

. . . he informed me that he had "pretty much made up his mind to be annihilated"; but still he does not seem to rest in that anticipation; and, I think, will never rest until he gets hold of a definite belief. It is strange how he persists—and has persisted ever since I·knew him, and probably long before—in wandering to-and-fro over these deserts, as dismal and monotonous as the sand hills amid which we were sitting. He can neither believe, nor be comfortable in his unbelief; and he is too honest and courageous not to try to do one or the other. If he were a religious man, he would be one of the most truly religious and reverential; he has a very high and noble nature, and better worth immortality than most of us.[2]

Coming from the friend with whom he had talked most intimately about such matters, this expression of wonder at Melville's obsession with religious problems is a classic statement of Melville's spiritual condition during the latter half of his life.

Certainly his is one of the strangest and most pathetic cases in his century. None of the English men of letters affected by the skepticism of the time, such as Clough and Arnold, were hit quite so hard by their disillusionment. And in comparison with Melville, most of the eminent American authors of his day found happy answers to their

1. Superior numbers throughout this and the following chapters refer to correspondingly numbered notes beginning on p. 127.

questions. Emerson and Thoreau, with their transcendental theories, and Longfellow, Lowell, and Holmes, with their Unitarian views, were relatively contented and optimistic. Whittier was a good Quaker. Whitman's worship of the universe buoyed him. Even Hawthorne, often morose on the problem of sin, was contented enough in his beliefs to pity Melville.

Yet it would have been odd if Melville had not given a great deal of thought to religious matters. His inherited theological cast of mind and the religious atmosphere that he was reared in would have made indifference on his part out of the ordinary. To get an insight into the God-fearing tradition he was born into, one has only to look at some of the letters and other documents that his Dutch Reformed and Congregationalist ancestors wrote about their everyday affairs and the crises common to all family life.

The Calvinistic tradition had been established on both sides of the family generations before Melville was born. His great-great-grandfather Melville served nearly half a century as a clergyman in the Scotch Kirk, a fact in which the family took much pride.[3] Melville's grandfather, the American-born Thomas Melville, was intended for the ministry and studied divinity at Princeton for over a year; but then, after visiting relatives in Scotland and England, he decided to become a merchant.[4] He remained a religious man, however, and he married a very devout woman.[5] Melville's grandfather General Peter Gansevoort was less religious-minded than his wife, Catherine Van Schaick, but he had faith in God and attended church.[6] Numerous letters show what an ardent Christian his wife was and what a deep impression her religion made on her children.[7]

H. V. Routh says that to Carlyle's father "an idea was something which concerned man's relation to God."[8] The same remark might be applied to Melville's father, for Allan Melville saw in everything the hand of a benevolent but jealous God. One of the numerous references to the

Deity in his letters reveals this clearly: ". . . that divine first cause, who always moulds events to subserve the purposes of mercy & wisdom, often subjects poor human nature to the severest trials, that he may better display his sovereign power. . . ."[9] To show his reverence and humility, he always wrote *God* with three capital letters.

Since one of his sons was to write a novel about a blasphemous Captain Ahab, it is noteworthy that Allan Melville himself was never more worshipful than when at sea. On one of his voyages he wrote to his wife that, owing to the seasickness of the only clergyman on board, the captain had asked him to conduct the services on the Sabbath and he had complied. "Indeed," he continued, "if men are ever seriously inclined, or feel their total & immediate dependence on GOD, it must be on an element where his most wonderful power is displayed, & where his omnipotence alone can save from destruction."[10] His trust in God gave him hope in financial disaster, and just before his death he was still firm in the belief that Providence would guide him to success.[11]

Fénelon's *Treatise on the Education of Daughters,* a copy of which Allan Melville owned,[12] advises teaching religious principles to children when they are very young; and *Justina,* a long didactic novel that his wife read aloud to one of their daughters, ends with the statement that parents who teach their offspring Christian doctrines will be able to stand before the throne of God on Judgment Day and "say with humble confidence, 'Here am I, O Lord! and the children that thou hast given me.' "[13] Allan Melville and his wife assumed the responsibility they felt as guardians of young souls. In addition to instructing their children at home, they took them regularly to church services to hear the word of God.[14] Before Allan Melville's death in 1832, his son Herman, then in his thirteenth year, had had time to learn a great deal about his father's religious views.*

---

* In *Pierre* Melville may have had his own father in mind when he wrote satirically that to Pierre's father "all gentlemanhood was vain; all claims to

He was subjected to his mother's influence, of course, for many more years. As a daughter of the illustrious and well-to-do General Peter Gansevoort, and as the wife of a highly respected gentleman who until just before his death was a successful businessman, Maria Melville had understandable pride in her worldly position; and yet her religion kept her aware, as she put it, "How uncertain & changing are all things here below. . . ."[15] The records of the First Dutch Reformed Church of Albany show that just after her husband's death she became a member of that church by profession of faith.[16] She kept up the Christian observances in her household. Mrs. Eleanor Melville Metcalf says that when her mother, Herman Melville's daughter, went to visit Mrs. Maria Melville in later years, ". . . family prayers were held, and the Sabbath was strictly kept. All frivolous books, sewing, knitting, or any other handiwork, were put away and religious tracts took their place. They had a cold dinner and attended church twice."[17] There is no reason to believe that the observances were less strict when young Herman was growing into manhood. As to his schooling, the Albany Academy, which he entered in 1830, was "a God-fearing school."[18]

The partly autobiographical *Pierre* tells us that at the age of sixteen Pierre joined the church.[19] The records of the church that Mrs. Maria Melville joined show that her daughters Helen and Augusta became members in 1837 and 1838, both, like their mother, by profession of faith; but the records contain nothing about Herman or his brothers. Whether or not Melville actually became a member of the church, he felt its influences. According to all the evidence, *Pierre* is in essence autobiographically true in saying that Pierre unconsciously accepted the faith of his fathers; and

it preposterous and absurd, unless the primeval gentleness and golden humanities of religion had been so thoroughly wrought into the complete texture of the character, that he who pronounced himself gentleman, could also assume the meek, but kingly style of Christian" (p. 6).

so is *Redburn* in representing its young hero as feeling strange without a church to go to on board ship, and as going to church almost every Sunday in Liverpool.[20]   *Typee* and *Omoo* of course are not exact records of Melville's life in the South Seas; but without proof to the contrary there is little reason to doubt his assertion, as the narrator in *Omoo*, that he attended a good many times the native churches under the control of the missionaries.[21]   As to Melville's connection with the church later, after he had written much about Christianity in his books, his journal of 1849-1850 shows that he went to church on six of the seven Sundays he spent in England.[22]   From the eighteen-fifties on, however, he seldom went to church.   Mrs. Metcalf writes: "He would on rare occasions go to All Souls' Church in Fourth Avenue [his wife's church], but for many years during the latter part of his life he did not do even this."[23]

After his own deflection from the church had begun, Melville continued to be closely associated with devout people.   His Unitarian wife found much consolation in her church and in the words of her pastor, the well-known Dr. Henry W. Bellows.   A sermon by Dr. Bellows inspired her to write the following lines, based on II Timothy 4:7, on a piece of paper that she kept folded in her Bible:

> "Hold on," my soul, with courage for the "fight"
> "Hold out," my feet, the weary "course" to run
> "Hold fast," my faith, bring patience to the "rack"—
> Oh God, thou knowest each hour of need! Look down,
> Give thine own help for courage, strength and faith,
> Or never may we win the victor's waiting crown.[24]

Various bookmarks, pressed four-leaf clovers and bits of fern, newspaper clippings, and unattached notes in her Bible indicate that she kept it by her constantly.   She marked it in a way to show her trust in love and faith, but verses on the endurance of hardship are especially marked.[25]   On a flyleaf she transcribed from Thomas à Kempis: "If thou bear the Cross, the Cross also will bear thee."   Her faith in God is clearly expressed in one of her letters: "The ways of Providence are indeed inscrutable and past finding out, but I am one of those who cling to the belief that some how these mysterious dispensations will seem right to us, and 'at even tide there shall be light.' "[26] Melville's sisters, who lived with him and his wife for a time, took an active part in church affairs; and Augusta, the one who aided him as a copyist, taught a Bible class.[27] His brothers, Allan and Tom, were similarly disposed toward the church;[28] Allan served as a vestryman in the Episcopal Church, and upon his death his bishop wrote a tribute to his character in a letter to his family.[29] Other details about Herman Melville's relatives might be cited, such as that his friendly, munificent father-in-law was a pewholder in a Unitarian church.[30] More will be said later of Melville's friendship with the good Episcopalians Evert and George Duyckinck, in New York, and the Morewoods, in Pittsfield.

The sturdy faith of Melville's family and some of his friends can hardly be overemphasized as an influence on his religious thought. Their belief in life after death, their conviction that God controls all for the best, were ever-present reminders of his earlier unquestioning faith. His envy of the religious peace enjoyed by those about him made him seek to strengthen what remained of his old faith, or to find a new faith to take the place of the old.

One of the earliest liberalizing influences on Melville's thought was the experience that he gained through traveling. The sights that he saw on his voyage to Liverpool and especially during the years in the South Seas did much toward making him question the creeds and principles that Christendom lived by. He showed when he wrote *Typee* and *Omoo* that what he had seen had convinced him that some people would have been better off if they had never heard of Jesus Christ. He had learned a great deal about the incompetence and even insincerity of many who professed to guide others to Christian salvation.

Soon after his return from the South Seas, in 1844, he began to read extensively, a fact which brings up the question of how much he was influenced by his reading. The purpose of this study is to analyze Melville's religious thought and only incidentally to try to point out the effect of his reading on his thought. Although it is possible to say when he read certain authors, and also to determine something of their influence upon him, one cannot be sure just how much he knew about many authors he mentioned or when he became acquainted with them. On the one hand, he may have read several volumes by an author and yet never have made a direct reference to him: Carlyle is not mentioned by name in any of Melville's published writings, but Evert Duyckinck's list of "Books Lent" shows that Melville borrowed several volumes of Carlyle's works.* On the other hand, Melville might have mentioned an author several times without having done any more than read about him, though of course from good secondary sources he could have got sound information about the ideas of many important figures.

The problem of chronology is also baffling. To take one example: The New York Public Library recently acquired for its Gansevoort-Lansing Collection an old school book entitled *The English Reader* in which "H. Melvill" is written in several places (when Melville was a child, the name was still spelled without the final *e*). There are no dates in the book, but one assumes that Melville studied it when he was a boy. Whoever the editor was—the title page is lost—he believed in setting moral and religious ideas before his youthful readers. The general tone of the book is indicated by the predominance among the prose selections

---

* See Duyckinck's "Books Lent," in a notebook in the Duyckinck Collection in the New York Public Library. The names of books lent by Duyckinck to Melville may also be found in Luther S. Mansfield, *Herman Melville: Author and New Yorker, 1844-51* (doctoral dissertation at the University of Chicago, 1936), chap. viii, and Willard Thorp, *Herman Melville: Representative Selection* . . (New York, 1938), pp. xxvii-xxviii, n.

of pieces from Blair on such subjects as "The dignity of virtue amidst corrupt examples," "The slavery of vice," and "The good man's comfort in affliction." Selections from Thomson, Pope, Young, and others set forth the argument from design for a beneficent Deity. Among the dialogues are Lord Lyttleton's "Locke and Bayle" ("Christianity defended against the cavils of scepticism") and Fénelon's "Democritus and Heraclitus." There is a piece by Addison on the immortality of the soul, and there are selections from Milton and Cowper. Did the readings in this volume make lasting impressions on the youthful Melville? Did he later read a great deal more by the authors represented here? If so, when?

Though ideally, of course, all of Melville's reading should be considered chronologically along with the development of his thought, lack of specific evidence about much of his reading makes it seem unwise to attempt such a procedure in this instance. The effect of certain authors on him will be considered later. But here, with little regard for chronology, a brief, informal survey of his reading in religion and philosophy seems pertinent simply as an indication of the breadth of his interest in those subjects.

The book that Melville knew longest and best was the Bible. His home training early acquainted him with it as revealed truth; and later he came to appreciate its beauty as literature and its "invaluable lessons of style," to use a phrase about it that he underlined in Arnold's *Essays in Criticism*.[31] His vast number of scriptural references and allusions show how familiar he was with the text. Miss Nathalia Wright estimates that two thirds of the six hundred and fifty references she noted in Melville's prose works are to the Old Testament, a fact of interest in connection with his pessimism.[32] The books traditionally ascribed to Solomon especially appealed to him, since they revealed "deeper and deeper and unspeakable meanings" on each reading.[33]

The text or texts of the Old Testament that Melville used have apparently been lost; but the copy of the New Testament and Psalms given to him in 1846 by his Aunt Jean has been preserved.[34] It is marked in a way to show careful reading. Just when Melville read the volume is not known—possibly at various times through several years. The profound influence on his idealism of the teachings of Christ did not prevent Melville's marking the text critically. Although most of the markings indicate approbation or ordinary interest, a few are noteworthy for other reasons. One annotation, for instance, gives a rather surprising interpretation to a remark made by Christ. The third time that Christ returns from praying and finds his Disciples sleeping, he says, according to Matthew 26:45: "Sleep on now, and take your rest. . . ." Melville underlined these words and annotated: "This is ironical." He violently objected to John's prophecy, in the last chapter of Revelation, that "if any man shall take away from the words of the book of this prophecy, God shall take away his part out of the book of life, and out of the holy city. . . ." Melville drew several heavy lines through this verse; but later he erased them. He also wrote and erased an annotation on John 13:29, which says that some of the Disciples misunderstood a remark that Christ made to Judas.* Some of the other markings and annotations will be taken up in later chapters.

Observations in Melville's works testify to his study of scriptural commentaries and to his knowledge of different versions of the Bible.[35] In his copy of Mackay's *The Book of English Songs* a stanza editorially added to a song caused him to annotate: "This is like the interpolations in the Song of Solomon. The original verses are full of nature & truth."[36] He marked in his *Shelley Memorials* a passage questioning the accuracy with which the biographers of Jesus recorded his life and sayings.[37] It may be significant that

* Mrs. Metcalf has assured me that her grandmother, Melville's wife, was too much in awe of her husband's genius to change or mar any words that he wrote.

in his copy of the New Testament and Psalms Melville marked only one verse in the Gospel of Mark, who, like Luke, was traditionally supposed to have known Jesus only at second hand, whereas he marked many verses in the other three Gospels. He was profoundly troubled by his reading of Strauss's *Life of Jesus*.[38]

Numerous references show his interest in various interpreters of Christian doctrine. He referred to Augustine on original sin,[39] he wrote familiarly of both Luther and Melanchthon,[40] and he had been brought up on Calvin. His library contained such diverse doctrinal opinions as may be found in John Taylor's *The Scripture Doctrine of Original Sin* and *A Summary View of the . . . Shakers*, the latter of which he bought in 1850 on a visit to the Shaker community in Hancock, Massachusetts.[41]

Literary taste as well as religious interest made him fond of certain seventeenth-century clergymen. One of the books that he borrowed from Evert Duyckinck in the late eighteen-forties and early eighteen-fifties was Fuller's book of characters, *The Holy State and the Profane State*. His reading of Burton's *The Anatomy of Melancholy* made him speak rather surprisingly of "old Burton as atheistical—in the exquisite irony of his passages on some sacred matters."[42] To Bunyan, he said, God had given "the pale, poetic pearl."[43] It is not unlikely that he read some of the sermons he referred to by Massillon, Tillotson, and Jeremy Taylor.[44] But perhaps more beloved by Melville than any of these worthies was Sir Thomas Browne, whom he once called a "crack'd Archangel."[45]

For Melville's reading of an author at the opposite pole from Browne, one has only to consider his purchase of Pierre Bayle's *Dictionary* in the spring of 1849 and his statement that he intended to spend his summer with the huge volumes.[46] A gentler skeptic whom Melville admired was Montaigne; his implication that there is a "right meaning" to Montaigne which many people do not get suggests that he felt pretty sure of his own understanding.[47]   Several references to Voltaire indicate his familiarity with that brilliant critic of Christianity.[48]   He had ample opportunity to become acquainted with the irreverence of another Frenchman in the volumes of Rabelais that he borrowed from Duyckinck.   He of course knew the arguments against Christianity of the Deists, among whom he mentioned Paine, Volney, Lord Herbert of Cherbury, and Ethan Allen.[49]

The great poets were important teachers for Melville. The deep impression that Dante made on him is reflected especially in *Pierre*.[50]   His knowledge of Spenser, whom Milton called "a better teacher than Aquinas," is attested by his use of several quotations from *The Faerie Queen*.[51] He made numerous references to Milton; and he significantly marked passages in his copy of Shelley's *Essays* which relate to anti-Christian argument in *Paradise Lost*.[52]   In 1849, when he really came to know Shakespeare, he found him "full of sermons-on-the-mount"; and in later life he wrote:

> No utter surprise can come to him
> Who reaches Shakespeare's core;
> That which we seek and shun is there—
> Man's final lore.[53]

Melville studied human nature in all kinds of writers. Before his "discovery" of Shakespeare, he showed that he knew something of Rousseau; and Rousseau's *Confessions* was among the books that he bought in 1849-50.[54]   Later, when he had grown more pessimistic about the nature of man, he referred to such authors as Machiavelli, Hobbes, Franklin, Tacitus, and Rochefoucauld on man.[55]

How he became acquainted with various philosophical ideas is, in this study, of less importance than the fact that he was acquainted with them.   Plato, who is far more frequently mentioned in his works than any other philosopher, represented a tradition that played a significant part in Melville's thinking.   The famous dialogue on immortality, the

Phaedo, was one of the two volumes that Melville said he
would hold in his hands to keep his balance over Bayle.[56]
As for ancient Neoplatonists, he seems to have made no
direct reference to Plotinus, though he used his name for
the "philosopher" in *Pierre,* but he mentioned Proclus in two
novels.[57]   He came on Platonic and Neoplatonic ideas of
course in innumerable sources.

Among the Stoics he paid especially high tribute to
Seneca; with lavish praise he incorporated into the text of
Mardi precepts from Seneca on the good life.[58]   He also
referred to Zeno, Marcus Aurelius, and Epictetus (and
Arrian, the collector of his sayings), and in his New Testament he wrote the Stoic poet Aratus's name by an allusion
of St. Paul's.[59]   Having been brought up in the Christian
tradition, Melville was naturally attracted to much in the
Platonic and Stoic philosophers.   Among other ancient philosophers and moralists whose names appear in his works are
Aristotle, Cicero, and Plutarch.[60]

Of the seventeenth-century philosophers, he knew something of the utilitarian philosophy of Bacon[61] and the mystical, pantheistic philosophy of Spinoza.   Though he rejected
Spinoza's philosophy, he appreciated it as one of the great
systems.[62]   He praised Hobbes's style, calling him a "para-
gon of perspicuity," and wrote of Hobbes's "mental habits"
as though he knew a good deal about them.[63]   He mentioned
Locke familiarly, in one instance commenting on his well-
known theory about the human mind at birth.[64]   And he
praised Hume's skepticism in a way to show that he understood and admired it.   He marked heavily a passage in
Schopenhauer saying that "From every page of David Hume
there is more to be learned than from the collected philosophical works of Hegel, Herbart, and Schleiermacher
together."[65]

In the introduction to *The World as Will and Idea* he
also marked a passage on the importance of Kant,[66] whose
name appears many times in Melville's works. Kant, Hegel,

and Schlegel were among the philosophers that Melville
and the lexicographer Adler discussed.[67]   Sundermann says
that although Melville knew some of the chief features of
Kant's philosophy, no profound influence is traceable in Melville's works.[68]   An annotation in Melville's copy of *Literature and Dogma* may be to the point here.   He wrote
"True" by Arnold's assertion that "In the German mind, as
in the German language, there does seem to be something *splay*, something blunt-edged, unhandy, and infelici-
tous. . . ."[69]   Yet we know that Melville read Schopenhauer
with great interest.   At the end of his life he acquired seven
volumes of Schopenhauer's works, and he marked profusely
the four more popular volumes.*   The kinship of Melville
to this pessimist is indicated by many of the marked passages.

His interest in metaphysical and moral questions is suggested by references to various writers besides those already
mentioned.   He referred to Berkeley on matter, Edwards on
the will, and Priestley on necessity.[70]   He knew something
of Shaftesbury.[71]   A lightly erased annotation in his copy
of Madame de Staël's *Germany* shows that at one time in
his life he was repelled by what he called "the counting-
room philosophy of Paley,"[72] who was so long popular with
the pious.   He mentioned Condorcet and even Abraham
Tucker.[73]

In turning to authors of previous ages for learning and
wisdom to help him out of his confusion, Melville was like
the majority of his contemporaries; but he also read many
authors of his own day and of the immediate past.   Some
of these of course have already been mentioned.   He bought
Goethe's *Autobiography* and *Letters from Italy* while abroad

---

* The four more popular volumes, translated by T. B. Saunders, are:
Religion: A Dialogue, and Other Essays (2d ed.; London, 1890) ; *Counsels
and Maxims* . . . (London, 1890) ; *The Wisdom of Life* . . . (2d ed.; London, 1891) ; and *Studies in Pessimism* (London, 1891).   The other three
volumes comprise *The World as Will and Idea*, trans. R. B. Haldane and J.
Kemp (The English Foreign and Philosophical Library; London, 1888-1890)
(H.C.L.).

in 1849-50, and soon afterwards borrowed *Wilhelm Meister* from Duyckinck. He appreciated Goethe's genius though he made fun of some of his ideas.[74] He borrowed *Sartor Resartus* and other works by Carlyle from Duyckinck in 1850. He made several familiar references to Coleridge, and recorded in one of his journals a talk with Adler in which Coleridge's religious views figured; he seems to have been more interested in Coleridge's prose than his poetry.[75]

He knew the other major Romantic poets, and his religious thought may have been more affected by some of their views than at first would seem likely. Although the "gentle and sequestered Wordsworth" had little effect on him,[76] the influence of Byron's Titanism in Melville's works is clear enough.[77] Melville knew a good deal of Shelley's poetry and prose; the markings in Melville's copies of Shelley's *Essays* and the *Shelley Memorials* show interest in a number of items, such as the "Essay on Christianity."[78]

Much of the religious perplexity of the middle of the century he found epitomized in Tennyson's *In Memoriam*, which he borrowed from Duyckinck in 1850. Thoreau's *A Week on the Concord and Merrimack Rivers*, which he also borrowed, contained thought that might have interested him, especially the chapter headed "Sunday." How soon he read Emerson is still a problem; but he was given a copy of Emerson's *Poems* in 1859, and in the sixties and seventies he acquired three volumes of Emerson's essays. The annotations and markings in these books reveal that although he considered Emerson a great person in many respects, he thought him intellectually arrogant and particularly objected to his easy disposal of the problem of evil.[79] The appeal of Hawthorne's views for Melville is attested by various well-known records of their friendship.[80] Apparently there is no evidence of what Melville thought of Sylvester Judd's queer transcendental novel *Margaret*, which he borrowed in 1850. He made comments of a religious nature, however, on books generally not thought of as inspiring such comment. When he was reviewing *The Oregon Trail*, Parkman's contemptuous attitude toward the Indians set Melville to proclaiming that as the sons of God all men, regardless of color, are brothers.[81] And about half of his review of Cooper's *The Sea Lions* is devoted to discussing rather satirically the religious elements in that novel; Cooper's psalm-singing, tight-fisted Deacon Pratt might well have influenced the conception of Captain Bildad in *Moby-Dick*.[82]

Melville's interest in Arnold is scarcely more than one would have expected. Various marked passages in the volumes of Arnold that he owned suggest harmony of thought between the two men on a number of religious and philosophical points.* The pessimism of the nineteenth-century James Thomson, some of whose works an English admirer sent him, pleased him much more than the excessive optimism that he found in many writers of his day.[83] He also wrote sympathetically of the gloomy Italian poet Leopardi, whose "theme is everywhere the mockery and wretchedness of this existence. . . ."[84]

Study of science of course also had its effect on Melville. It is not surprising that he referred to such famous scientists as Galileo, Newton, Buffon, LaPlace, Lyell, Darwin, and Agassiz, but he referred also to a great many less famous. He read and gave his opinion of numerous "authorities" on the subject of whales.[85] He was aware that geological discoveries disproved much in documents long accepted as true.[86] His appreciation of Darwin's importance is shown by the prominent place he gives Darwin in *Clarel*, where the effect of science on religion is seriously discussed.[87] The scientific analysis of legends about Rome by Niebuhr and of scriptural records by Strauss caused Melville to set

---

* *Essays in Criticism* (Boston, 1865), *New Poems* (Boston, 1867), *Literature and Dogma* (New York, 1881), *Mixed Essays, Irish Essays, and Others* (New York, 1883), and *Culture and Anarchy and Friendship's Garland* (New York, 1883).

down one of the most pathetic passages of despair that he ever wrote.[88]

Though he can hardly be said to have made a scientifically comparative study of religions, he was familiar at least in a general way with religions other than the Christian. What he wrote about Polynesian religion has won him a limited amount of prestige as an authority on that subject.[89] He had neither the knowledge of the oriental scriptures nor the reverence for them that Alcott, Emerson, and Thoreau had; but various references show that he knew something about Hinduism, Buddhism, and the Persian religions.[90] His references to Zoroastrianism, Manichaeism, and Parseeism are the more interesting because of his particular concern over evil; and the same may be said of passages mentioning the early Christian heretics, the Gnostics and the Marcionites.[91] One is not surprised to find in his works incidental references to Egyptian, Assyrian, Chinese, and Norse beliefs and an abundance of references to the Greek and Roman mythologies.[92] He evidently was much impressed by Lucian's irreverence toward the ancient deities.[93] He wrote of Mohammed and the Koran years before he went to the Holy Land, where he saw Mohammedanism in practice.[94] Numerous references indicate that his interest in the origins of Christianity led him to texts other than the (ld Testament in his study of the Hebrew religion.[95]

Even so general a survey suggests that Melville had a very wide interest in literature of a religious and philosophical nature. For a man who began to read extensively only after he had reached his middle twenties, he covered a great deal of territory. His reading both helped him to solve problems and gave rise to new problems. A close examination of the records of his thought reveals what some of his major problems were and the development of his attitude toward them.

CHAPTER II

VOYAGER INTO THE "WORLD OF MIND"

WHEN MELVILLE read in his New Testament St. Paul's counsel to the Romans, "Hast thou faith? Have it to thyself before God,"[1] he annotated, "The only kind of faith— one's own." And the strongest faith, he felt, is one that has been stripped of all superfluities. He made a not uncommon defense of skepticism in the chapter on "Faith and Knowledge" in *Mardi* (1849) when he wrote: "The higher the intelligence, the more faith, and the less credulity: Gabriel rejects more than we, but out-believes us all."[2]

Many passages in *Mardi* show that Melville set a high value on reason. During the tour of the world represented by the archipelago called Mardi, it is significant that Babbalanja, the philosopher, does most of the talking. His views and those of the ancient sage Bardianna, whom he so reverently quotes, are especially important as affording insight into ideas that Melville entertained. A quotation from Bardianna may be cited as giving some of Melville's own views on reason during this period:

Undeniably, reason was the first revelation; and so far as it tests all others, it has precedence over them. It comes direct to us, without suppression or interpolation; and with Oro's [God's] indisputable imprimatur. But inspiration though it be, it is not so arrogant as some think. Nay, far too humble, at times it submits to the grossest indignities. Though in its best estate, not infallible; so far as it goes, for us, it is reliable. When at fault, it stands still. We speak not of visionaries. But if this our first revelation stops short of the uttermost, so with all others. If, often, it only perplexes: much more the rest. They leave much unexpounded; and disclosing new mysteries, add to the enigma.[3]

A number of ideas expressed here deserve particular note. Reason is divine: it comes direct from God. Having priority over other "revelations," it may be used to test the Scriptures. "Nor is there any impiety," says Babbalanja elsewhere, "in the right use of our reason, whatever the issue."[4] Because of its humility reason submits to base indignities: ". . . shall we employ it but for a paw, to help us to our bodily needs, as the brutes use their instinct?"[5] As visionaries are ruled out, the passage cannot be considered a plea for uncontrolled mysticism. The reason referred to here is the intuitive reason of Plato ("inspiration" is used as a synonym for it in one sentence). It is, in a general sense, the reason of Kant or Coleridge as opposed to the understanding.

When Melville wrote to Hawthorne, "Until I was twenty-five, I had no development at all,"[6] he was obviously referring to the life of the mind that he had entered upon soon after his return from the South Seas, in 1844. His first two books tell comparatively little of this new course that he had taken, but his third does. The following autobiographical passage in *Mardi* is significant:

Oh, reader, list! I've chartless voyaged. With compass and the lead, we had not found these Mardian Isles. Those who boldly launch, cast off all cables; and turning from the common breeze, that's fair for all, with their own breath fill their own sails. Hug the shore, naught new is seen; and 'Land ho!' at last was sung, when a new world was sought.

That voyager steered his bark through seas untracked before; ploughed his own path mid jeers; though with a heart that oft was heavy with the thought that he might only be too bold, and grope where land was none.

So I.

And though essaying but a sportive sail, I was driven from my course by a blast resistless; and ill-provided, young, and bowed to the brunt of things before my prime, still fly before the gale;—hard have I striven to keep stout heart.

And if it harder be than e'er before to find new climes, when now our seas have oft been circled by ten thousand prows,—much more the glory!

But this new world here sought is stranger far than his, who stretched his vans from Palos. It is the world of mind; wherein the wanderer may gaze round, with more of wonder than Balboa's band roving through the golden Aztec glades.

But fiery yearnings their own phantom-future make, and deem it present. So, after all these fearful, fainting trances, the verdict be, the golden haven was not gained;—yet, in bold quest thereof, better to sink in boundless deeps, than float on vulgar shoals; and give me, ye gods, an utter wreck, if wreck I do.[7]

Once tried, he says, the life of reasoning so fascinated him that he was resolved to continue looking for truth by this means even though he sometimes suspected that his efforts would come to nought, or, worse, would end disastrously for him. His self-consciousness in his new, heroic role is quite apparent. The use of exploring the seas to symbolize exploring the mind for undiscovered truth is common in Melville's works. There is an important passage in *Moby-Dick* (1851) written in the same vein as that just quoted from *Mardi:*

Glimpses do ye seem to see of that mortally intolerable truth; that all deep, earnest thinking is but the intrepid effort of the soul to keep the open independence of her sea; while the wildest winds of heaven and earth conspire to cast her on the treacherous, slavish shore?

But as in landlessness alone resides the highest truth, shoreless, indefinite as God—so, better is it to perish in that howling infinite, than be ingloriously dashed upon the lee, even if that were safety! For worm-like, then, oh! who would craven crawl to land![8]

The land represents empirical truth. Melville here expresses the philosophical view that one must shut this kind of truth out of his mind if he is to indulge in the introspective abstract reasoning, necessarily general, which discloses reality.

But a year later, in *Pierre* (1852), Melville takes a slightly different view of "profound and fearless thought."

He says that it leads to regions of "rarefied atmosphere" where the thinker sees "the most immemorially admitted maxims of men begin to slide and fluctuate, and finally become wholly inverted. . . ." Sad examples of too adventurous minds teach us "that it is not for man to follow the trail of truth too far, since by so doing he entirely loses the directing compass of his mind; for arrived at the Pole, to whose barrenness only it points, there, the needle indifferently respects all points of the horizon alike."[9] At the time of writing *Pierre* Melville had indulged in introspective reasoning to excess. In *Mysticism: A Study in the Nature and Development of Man's Spiritual Consciousness*, Evelyn Underhill writes: "The fully developed and completely conscious soul can open as an anemone does, and *know* the ocean in which she is bathed."[10] Melville used a similar figure in regard to his own growth. In the letter saying that his development had begun when he was twenty-five, he added: "Three weeks have scarcely passed, at any time between then and now [from 1844 to 1851], that I have not unfolded within myself. But I feel that I am now come to the inmost leaf of the bulb, and that shortly the flower must fall to the mould."[11]

His following the course of reasoning to the point where he could make such a gloomy prediction of himself is strange in view of his awareness all along that one should temper speculation with recourse to the normal life of the mind and the emotions. Early in this period Melville had expressed an opinion that the greatest wisdom for man lies in following the dictates of the heart—the emotions that make one benevolent toward his fellow men, the intuitions that cause one to rejoice in moral beauty. Several passages in *Mardi* indicate his reverence for the life of the heart. In one of the most important of these Babbalanja says that within "our hearts is all we seek; though in that search many need a prompter. Him I have found in Alma," or Christ.[12] The old man of Serenia who sets forth Melville's

Christian ideals says that Christ "but opens unto us our own hearts."[13] He affirms that Christ is the perfect embodiment of "right reason," that function of the mind which enables man to live according to the ethical laws decreed by God (as used here, "right reason" seems comparable to "practical reason" as opposed to "speculative reason").[14] Like Pascal, Melville felt that "The Heart has its Reasons, which Reason doth not comprehend. . . ."[15] It is significant that Melville copied on a flyleaf of his New Testament and Psalms the following quotation from Saint Évremond: "Who well considers the Christian religion, would think that God meant to keep it in the dark from our understandings, and make it turn upon the motions of our hearts."[16] One of Melville's letters showed that if there were any danger that the heart and the head could not work together, Melville stood "for the heart. To the dogs with the head!"[17] In *Pierre* he had his hero exclaim that "the brains grow maggoty without a heart; but the heart's the preserving salt itself, and can keep sweet without the head."[18]

Melville's ideal was a happy union of the heart and the head. In his copy of *Mosses from an Old Manse*, in which he underlined "Thought grows mouldy," he also heavily marked a passage referring to "such light as never illuminates the earth, save when a great heart burns as the household fire of a grand intellect."[19] And in the letter to Hawthorne just mentioned above he said in regard to "Ethan Brand":

It is a frightful poetical creed that the cultivation of the brain eats out the heart. But it's my *prose* opinion that in most cases, in those men who have fine brains and work them well, the heart extends down to the hams. And though you smoke them with the fire of tribulation, yet, like veritable hams, the head only gives the richer and better flavour.[20]

But Melville's conciliation of the two was not so successful as he wished it to be. Study of his religious thought reveals a dichotomy that caused him much distress. **Trying** to unite the heart and the head in order to find truth which would give him religious peace was a lifelong problem for him. He realized that the question What is truth? "is more final than any answer,"[21] but this realization did not keep him from looking for an answer that would come nearer to satisfying him than any of the compromises devised by other men.

The question at the bottom of his reasoning concerned the nature of God. As a son of the Calvinistic Allan Melville, who saw the hand of God in everything, Melville naturally gave much thought to the subject. He had little to say about it in *Typee* and *Omoo*, but *Mardi* plainly shows how it perplexed him.

He expressed no doubt at this time about the being of the Deity. "God is my Lord," he says emphatically; "and though many satellites revolve around me, I and all mine revolve round the great central Truth, sun-like, fixed, and luminous forever in the foundationless firmament."[22] The general tone of *Mardi* makes one feel that Babbalanja speaks for Melville when he asserts that "atheists there are none. For in things abstract, men but differ in the sounds that come from their mouths, and not in the wordless thoughts lying at the bottom of their beings."[23] Although there is no doubt about Melville's theism, it is not so easy to say just what he believed in regard to the nature of the Deity. He thought argument over the trinitarian conception of God rather foolish, since one might be divided into any number of parts.[24] He was attracted by the idea that "to Himself His own universe is He."[25] During and just after writing *Moby-Dick* he wrote to Hawthorne of having temporary pantheistic feelings.[26] But in spite of such moments he was not a pantheist in the Spinozistic sense.[27] While he thought of the universe as animated by the spirit of God, he looked upon God as transcendent also. The universe is "a Judea," with a timeless, ubiquitous, omnipotent God as "its head."[28]

In *Typee* God is referred to as a benevolent provider for the natives of the Marquesas, but not for the natives who shiver and starve among the wilds of Tierra-del-Fuego.[29] In *Mardi* the poet, Yoomy, says that God champions the right among men, but the philosopher, Babbalanja, argues that the Deity is often indifferent as to whether right or wrong prevails among men.[30]   Melville points to the heavenly constellations as declaring the glory of God, but he does not forget the shark: "As well hate a seraph as a shark. Both were made by the same hand."[31]   Melville had begun to worry as to why a benevolent Deity permits evil. He could not solve the problem so easily as some of his contemporaries.   Emerson, for instance, maintained that evil is merely the privation of good, as darkness is the privation of light, and that all tends toward ultimate good.[32]   There is an assertion in *Mardi* that "what seems evil to us may be good to" God,[33] but Melville found little comfort in the idea. He repeats, through Babbalanja, the old proposition of Epicurus: ". . . since evil abounds, and Oro [God] is all things, then he cannot be perfectly good; wherefore, Oro's omnipresence and moral perfection seems incompatible."[34] And he argues that it is vain to say evil exists because "a rebel angel" temporarily governs the world;[35] God has no viceroys; he himself rules continuously.   Belief in the infinite power of God and awareness of evil are responsible for the mournful query as to how God can "witness all this woe, and give no sign."[36]   The questioning of God's justice to man reaches a climax when Babbalanja asks an angel in a vision: ". . . why create the germs that sin and suffer, but to perish?"   The angel answers that this makes of God "the everlasting mystery he is. . . ."[37]   Melville's distress over the evil in the world can hardly be overemphasized as an influence on his reasoning about the Deity.

Another problem that concerned Melville is the question of man's divinity. One of the bases of his democracy was the idea that all men are "sprung from one head, and made in one image."[38] In *Moby-Dick* he reached rhetorical heights in proclaiming "that democratic dignity which, on all hands, radiates without end from God; Himself! The great God absolute! The centre and circumference of all democracy! His omnipresence, our divine equality!"[39] And he said in a rhapsodic letter to Hawthorne: "I feel that the Godhead is broken up like the bread at the Supper, and that we are the pieces. Hence this infinite fraternity of feeling."[40] But such passages do not tell the whole story. Melville believed that man is divine inasmuch as he is a part of a universe animated by the spirit of God, but whether man is peculiarly divine was another matter. There is evidence that Melville thought a good deal about the nature of this divinity in man. Babbalanja's assertion that "in his faculties, high Oro is but what a man would be, infinitely magnified," cannot be given much weight, since Babbalanja on another occasion suggests a rather damning celestial genealogy: "We are idiot, younger sons of gods, begotten in dotages divine; and our mothers all miscarry."[41] Nor does old Bardianna set man very high on the philosophical scale of being: "We are but a step in a scale, that reaches farther above us than below."[42] Poignant queries of characters in *Mardi*—"Have we angelic spirits?" "Are we angels, or dogs?"[43]—suggest a certain amount of perplexity on the part of the author himself.

Melville's Christian training was of course the most important influence on his thought about the divinity of man, and the marking of his New Testament and Psalms shows his interest in scriptural testimony on the subject. He marked the verse in which Christ tells the multitude, "And call no man your father upon the earth: for one is your Father, which is in heaven,"[44] and the verse in which Christ tells the Disciples: ". . . it is not ye that speak, but the Spirit of your Father which speaketh in you."[45] He marked the Psalmist's praise of God for making man but "a little lower than the angels."[46]   One wonders what he thought of Paul's saying: "I think also that I have the spirit of God."[47] He underlined and wrote an annotation on the words "I think," but later he erased the annotation.   Paul's telling the Athenians: "as certain also of your own poets have said, For we are also his [God's] offspring,"[48] caused Melville to write in the margin: "Aratus," an annotation indicating that he knew the Stoic poet Aratus's *Phaenomena,* which opens with the assertion that men are the offspring of Zeus.

Another passage which interested him is the one in John saying:

Jesus answered them, Is it not written in your law, I said, Ye are gods?

If he called them gods, unto whom the word of God came, and the scripture cannot be broken;

Say ye of him, whom the Father hath sanctified, and sent unto the world, Thou blasphemest; because I said, I am the Son of God?[49]

An annotation on these verses refers to a flyleaf at the end of the volume.   There, in Melville's hand, is the following inscription for which no author is given:

If we can conceive it possible, that the creator of the world himself assumed the form of his creature, and lived in that manner for a time upon earth, this creature must seem to us of infinite perfection, because susceptible of such a combination with his maker.   Hence, in our idea of man there can be no inconsistency with our idea of God: and if we often feel a certain disagreement with Him and remoteness from Him, it is but the more on that account our duty, not like advocates of the wicked Spirit, to keep our eyes continually on the nakedness and wickedness of our nature; but rather to seek out every property and beauty, by which our pretension to a similarity with the Divinity may be made good.

Melville's writing this passage in his New Testament and Psalms emphasizes his fascination with the question of man's divinity, and shows his appreciation of a religious attitude that would develop the best in man.

According to the evidence as a whole, Melville believed that all men are possessed of a spark of divinity, but their sad condition troubled him, and he was sometimes pained by his awareness that there is no knowing this side of death whether, in the Christian sense, men are truly the children of God.[50]

If Melville had been able to convince himself, once and for all, that man has a divine and imperishable soul, he might have spared himself much unhappy reasoning about man's immortality. As it was, this was one of the subjects that occupied him most. The motto of the paternal side of his family, *Denique Caelum*—"Heaven at last"[51]—should have had a question mark after it so far as he was concerned.

He condemned the Calvinistic doctrines on immortality taught him in childhood.[52] Though he made more or less conventional references to hell, and though he knew that belief in hell gives perverse consolation to many who suffer on earth, he thought the myth of fiery persecution a "horrible fable": ". . . better we were all annihilated, than that one man should be damned."[53] His views on this point are interestingly revealed in the "Agatha" letter to Hawthorne, where Melville objects to a characterization "hinting of a future supplemental castigation."[54] And as for heaven, "Not one of Oro's priests telleth a straight story concerning it; 'twill be hard finding their paradises."[55] The buoyant prophecy that in heaven finally "Christian shall join hands between Gentile and Jew"[56] should be taken as evidence of Melville's democratic, brotherly love rather than as a statement of his belief in a corporeal afterlife; for he was amused at the idea of the resurrection of the body.[57]

"What it is to be immortal has not yet entered into our thoughts," says old Bardianna. "To live at all, is a high vocation; to live forever, and run parallel with Oro, may truly appal us."[58] The devout Father Mapple, in *Moby-Dick*, expresses a similar idea.[59] Bardianna condemns the notion that heaven will be a place of ease: ". . . if we live hereafter, it will not be in lyrics. . . . The eternity to come is but a prolongation of time present. . . ." He advocates a life of introspective reasoning, for "much of the knowledge we seek, already we have in our cores. . . . In solitude, let us exhume our ingots. Let us hear our own thoughts."[60] The influence of Platonic thought is obvious here, as it is later, in Babbalanja's vision.[61] Babbalanja dreams that in heaven the individual will "but put off lowly temporal pinings, for angel and eternal aspirations"; there "spiritual lives" will be "prolonged by fast keeping of the law of mind," and humility, or "confessed ignorance," will be rewarded by advancement into new realms of wisdom. But since only God "can know all," though heavenly beings "will for aye progress in wisdom and in good; yet, will they never gain a fixed beatitude."[62]

Even so, the chance for immortality is at best "but a hope."[63] Emerson, who finally gave up his belief in personal immortality, once asserted: "Our dissatisfaction with any other solution is the blazing evidence of immortality."[64] Melville in *Mardi* asked whether it does "not appear a little unreasonable to imagine, that there is any creature, fish, flesh, or fowl, so little in love with life, as not to cherish hopes of a future state." Allowing his humor to play on the idea, he concluded: "As for the possible hereafter of the whales; a creature eighty feet long without stockings, and thirty feet round the waist before dinner, is not inconsiderately to be consigned to annihilation."[65]

It is vain of man to think that in the eternal flux of nature he alone is permanent.[66] An idea advanced in Bishop Butler's *Analogy* is indicted in one of the arguments in *Mardi*. When Babbalanja is asked whether he considers the transformation of the larva into the butterfly "a fit illustration of the miraculous change to be wrought in man after death," he answers:

No; for the analogy has an unsatisfactory end. From its chrysalis state, the silkworm but becomes a moth, that very quickly expires. Its longest existence is as a worm. All vanity, vanity . . . to seek in nature for positive warranty to these aspirations of ours. Through all her provinces, nature seems to promise immortality to life, but destruction to beings.[67]

Tennyson is reported to have said in conversation, as he "grew crimson with excitement," that if immortality "be not true, then no God but a mocking fiend created us. . . . I'd bind my head to-night in a chloroformed handkerchief and have done with it all."[68] Melville had no such conviction as to God's being morally obligated to give happiness to man in another world for what he suffers in this one. To "make restitution implies a wrong; and Oro can do no wrong."[69] (In *The Confidence-Man* it is suggested that the doctrine of future retribution might be perversely interpreted to affirm "that Providence was not now, but was going to be.")[70] Moreover, Melville had little respect for "the counting-room philosophy" of Paley and others who taught that one should live a good life here because it will pay big dividends in the next world.[71] One of the reasons he admired Seneca is that Seneca taught the beauty of the good life itself: "And is it not more divine in this philosopher, to love righteousness for its own sake, than for pious sages to extol it as the means of everlasting felicity?"[72] Old Bardianna expresses Melville's finest spirit when he says: ". . . if, after all, we should be no more forever;—far better to perish meriting immortality than to enjoy it unmeritorious[ly]."[73]

Unfortunately, Melville could not let the matter rest at that. In the rhapsodic, "pantheistic" letter that he wrote to Hawthorne in 1851 he said, "Knowing you persuades me more than the Bible of our immortality";[74] but one observes that he uses the word *persuades* and not *convinces*. The question of whether man is immortal continued to vex him.

Man's moral nature was another subject of the first importance to Melville. Trained as a Calvinist, he had probably been taught that man himself was responsible for his impure moral condition. In a review of Hawthorne's *Mosses from an Old Manse* he referred to "that Calvinistic sense of Innate Depravity and Original Sin, from whose visitations, in some shape or other, no deeply thinking mind is always free," and said that "in certain moods, no man can weigh this world without throwing in something, somehow like Original Sin, to strike the uneven balance."[75] But the very looseness of his assertion that "in certain moods" one has to "throw in" something "somehow like" the doctrine of the fall indicates that, although he may have thought about the doctrine a great deal, he did not adhere to it. He made casual references to the fall,[76] but, as already stated, his reasoning points to the all-powerful Deity as responsible for the presence of both the evil and the good in the universe.

As to the evil in man's nature, he believed that some men's constitutions prevent their being good. Referring to the idea around which Holmes later wrote *Elsie Venner*, Babbalanja asks: ". . . if the instinctive passions through life naturally have the supremacy over the moral sense, as in extreme cases we see it developed in irreclaimable malefactors,—shall we pronounce such, criminal and detestable wretches?" His conclusion is that "it is easier for some men to be saints than for others not to be sinners."[77] In another instance he says: "[That a man] is not bad, is not of him. Potter's clay and wax are all moulded by hands invisible. The soil decides the man."[78] Although this strain of determinism, as will be shown later, is one of the most important elements in Melville's thought, it should not be taken to signify that Melville held human beings morally unaccountable. It simply indicates that he was more keenly aware than such a thinker as Emerson of the temperamental flaws that hamper man, and it helps explain why Melville, like Holmes, had a great pity for suffering mankind.

One can also find optimistic views on man in this early period. Like the Stoics, St. Paul, the Deists, and many others, Melville asserted that the moral laws are revealed to all men. The peaceful and friendly relationship of the Typees he attributed to "an inherent principle of honesty and charity toward each other," to the "universally diffused perception of what is *just* and *noble*. .. ." The natives "seemed to be governed by that sort of tacit commonsense law which, say what they will of the inborn lawlessness of the human race, has its precepts graven upon every breast."[79] In *Mardi* Bardianna affirms that "we need not be told what righteousness is; we were born with the whole Law in our hearts."[80] Some of the idealism in regard to primitive man in *Typee* and *Omoo* is almost certainly attributable to the influence of Rousseau,[81] but, as Thorp has observed, Melville was far from being "a naïve Rousseauist."[82]

From all that Melville said in his early works on the moral nature of man, free will, predestination, necessity, and the like, one can draw certain broad conclusions.[83] Melville admitted that some men are constitutionally unfitted to abide by moral principles, but he maintained that the mass of men can lead better lives if they use their faculties properly. Though they have some bad impulses, they also have good impulses, and they have the freedom to act upon these.

Melville's concern over the relationship of man to man and of man to God is obvious in much of his writing. Unlike many of his countrymen, Melville did not feel that men had to be converted to Christianity in order to maintain a highly ethical relationship. On the contrary, he had seen so much evil among men in lands nominally Christianized that he deplored the invasion of the South Sea islands by Western civilization though missionaries were among the first to move in. He affirmed that the natives of the Typee valley lived on better terms than many peoples who repeated the Lord's Prayer every night. Mere nominal conversion to Christianity did the islanders no good, and the evils that accompanied it did them both moral and physical harm.[84]

The significant place that Melville gives in *Mardi* to a book by a "heathen" author throws much light on his own ideas about ethics and religion. Babbalanja comes by chance upon *A Happy Life,* by an anonymous pagan author, and reads from it to the other travelers. What Melville does here is simply to quote a passage, in condensed form and with minor changes, from Seneca's *Morals:*

I would bear the same mind, whether I be rich or poor, whether I get or lose in the world. I will reckon benefits well placed as the fairest part of my possession, not valuing them by number or weight, but by the profit and esteem of the receiver; accounting myself never the poorer for anything I give. What I do shall be done for conscience, not ostentation. I will eat and drink, not to gratify my palate, but to satisfy nature. I will be cheerful to my friends, mild and placable to my enemies. I will prevent an honest request, if I can foresee it; and I will grant it, without asking. I will look upon the whole world as my country; and upon Oro [God] both as the witness and the judge of my words and my deeds. I will live and die with this testimony: that I loved a good conscience; that I never invaded another man's liberty; and that I preserved my own. I will govern my life and my thoughts, as if the whole world were to see the one, and to read the other; for what does it signify, to make anything a secret to my neighbour, when to Oro all our privacies are open.[85]

One of the travelers asks whether these sentences, together with a few more quoted, are not from the sayings of Alma. Babbalanja answers that they are "from one, who though he lived ages ago, never saw, scarcely heard of Alma," and continues: ". . . that a mere man, and a heathen, in that most heathenish time, should give utterance to such heavenly wisdom, seems more wonderful than that an inspired prophet should reveal it." Though Babbalanja admits that he himself at this time wants more truth than any man can give him, the tribute he pays to Seneca's love of righteousness is all any moralist could wish:

. . . out of itself, Religion has nothing to bestow. Nor will she save us from aught, but from the evil in ourselves. Her one grand end is to make us wise; her only manifestations are reverence to Oro, and love to man; her only, but ample reward, herself. He who has this, has all. He who has this, whether he kneel to an image of wood, calling it Oro; or to an image of air, calling it the same; whether he fasts or feasts; laughs or weeps;—that man can be no richer. And this religion, faith, virtue, righteousness, good, whate'er you will, I find in this book I hold. No written page can teach me more.[86]

Aside from the attitude toward immortality and the absence of reference to Christ, the views on ethics and religion expressed here are fundamentally the same as those attributed to the inhabitants of Serenia, who represent Melville's ideal Christianity. The section of *Mardi* describing the life of these people is of the greatest importance for understanding Melville's ideas for this period on the relationship among men and between men and God. What Melville considered ideal in this respect, however, stands out in greater relief when set against his unfavorable criticism of Christianity.

When telling his readers, in *Typee* and *Omoo,* that the South Sea islanders would be better off without Christianity and all that went with it, Melville brought a number of charges against the missionaries. So much has already been published on this subject, however, by Anderson, Forsythe, and others,[87] that it seems unnecessary to do more here than to reiterate briefly Melville's chief criticisms.

Though *Typee* (1846) contained enough hostility toward the missionaries to stir up some ill feeling, and consequently was to be expurgated by the publishers Wiley and Putnam in its second edition, it was in *Omoo* (1847) that Melville went into detail in his criticism and documented his opinions with quotations from books by other travelers.

He granted the good intentions of the churches in sending out missionaries and admitted that the missionaries had done some good, as in translating the Bible into the native tongue and in lessening the evils caused by commerce with the whites.[88] But they had done less good than in the "glowing accounts"[89] sent home they claimed to have done, and they had done some harm. They had "denationalized" the natives, depriving them of their games and festivals, and thus had caused them to indulge the more in idleness and sensuality.[90] They had forced the natives to attend church, sometimes calling upon whippers delegated to assist in this.[91] They had often delivered sermons meant to entertain rather than to instruct in Christian living.[92] They had shown the worst kind of bigotry in fomenting hatred for other sects; Melville was harder on the Protestants for this than on the Catholic priests in Tahiti for their loose living.[93] All in all, the missionaries possessed many of the characteristics that made Melville inveigh against organized Christianity in several books besides *Typee* and *Omoo*.

In *Mardi* (1849) he continued with his criticism of some of the worst elements in institutions supposed to promote brotherhood and reverence for God. For an insight into Melville's unfavorable views of Christianity during the early years of his career, there is no better source than the portions of this book dealing with life on the isle of Maramma.

The monarchical government of Maramma is headed by a pontiff who owes his authority to the superstitious awe of his subjects. Though some of the pontiff's attributes may have been drawn from the papacy, Melville satirized in Maramma not merely Catholicism but the whole of organized Christianity. The island is full of social injustice, with the rich living near the miserable poor; Maramma champions slavery in southern Vivenza (the United States).[94]

The priesthood is represented by a blind guide who, though in private he gives vent to his doubt, publicly plays the hypocrite and persecutes even to death those who express disbelief in the doctrines of Maramma. He professes to be humble but proves arrogant. He says that man's needs are few, but makes extortionate demands on the pilgrims, draining the poor of all they have and yet exempting some of the smooth-tongued rich. Those who come to worship are as reprehensible and pathetic as their guide. One tries to buy salvation. One silently pretends to accept what he does not believe. Another thinks that profundity of faith is shown by believing the impossible. Still another declares that she leans on those considered wiser because she is afraid to think for herself.

The doctrines of Maramma are based to such an extent on authority supposedly derived from Alma that a discussion of this Mardian Christ between Babbalanja and Mohi, the historian, is worth quoting at length. Melville gives the historian's account in condensed form:

Alma, it seems, was an illustrious prophet, and teacher divine; who, ages ago, at long intervals, and in various islands, had appeared to the Mardians under the different titles of Brami, Manko, and Alma. Many thousands of moons had elapsed since his last and most memorable avatar, as Alma on the Isle of Maramma. Each of his advents had taken place in a comparatively dark and benighted age. Hence, it was devoutly believed, that he came to redeem the Mardians from their heathenish thrall; to instruct them in the ways of truth, virtue, and happiness; to allure them to good by promises of beatitude hereafter; and to restrain them from evil by denunciations of woe. Separated from the impurities and corruptions, which in a long series of centuries had become attached to everything originally uttered by the prophet, the maxims, which as Brami he had taught, seemed similar to those inculcated by Manko. But as Alma, adapting his lessons to the improved condition of humanity, the divine prophet had more completely unfolded his scheme; as Alma, he had made his last revelation.

This narration concluded, Babbalanja mildly observed, "Mohi: without seeking to accuse you of uttering falsehoods; since what you relate rests not upon testimony of your own; permit me, to question the fidelity of your account of Alma. The prophet came to dissipate errors, you say; but superadded to many that have survived the past, ten thousand others have originated in various constructions of the principles of Alma himself. The prophet came to do away all gods but one; but since the days of Alma, the idols of Maramma have more than quadrupled. The prophet came to make us Mardians more virtuous and happy; but along with all previous good, the same wars, crimes, and miseries, which existed in Alma's day, under various modifications are yet extant. Nay: take from your chronicles, Mohi, the history of those horrors, one way or other, resulting from the doings of Alma's nominal followers, and your chronicles would not so frequently make mention of blood. The prophet came to guarantee our eternal felicity; but according to what is held in Maramma, that felicity rests on so hard a proviso, that to a thinking mind, but very few of our sinful race may secure it. For one, then, I wholly reject your Alma; not so much because of all that is hard to be understood in his histories; as because of obvious and undeniable things all round us; which, to me, seem at war with an unreserved faith in his doctrines as promulgated here in Maramma. Besides, everything in this isle strengthens my incredulity; I never was so thorough a disbeliever as now."[95]

The people of Maramma believe in the tyranny of God and Christ and in the total depravity of man. Oro and Alma, they say, command that man grovel in the dust and "declare himself the vilest creature that crawls." They maintain that unbelievers are damned to eternal hell. Thousands of contradictory prayers rise in Maramma; and all the idols are somewhat mutilated as a result of hostility among the devotees. The dark, poisonous jungle of the island is in keeping with the unwholesome spiritual atmosphere.

A wholly different kind of life appears on the island where Melville's ideal Christians live. Here Melville resorts to different technique: the travelers do not see the life of this island, but are told about it by the gentle old man who greets them. In graphic quality this part of the narrative stands in about the same relationship to the part on Maramma as the *Paradiso* does to the *Inferno*.

In Serenia, the "land of Love," all human relationships and the relationship between man and God are based on the teachings of Christ,[96] but here these teachings are stripped clean of the corruptions of Maramma. The reference to Jesus in *Typee* as "divine and gentle"[97] implies that if Melville at the time of writing that book did not believe Christ to be supernatural, he at least profoundly admired him. In the section of *Mardi* on Maramma he indicts some of the worst elements in the worship of Christ through the centuries. In that on Serenia he indicates what Christ might mean to those who concentrated on the vital ideas in his teachings.

On this isle there is no monarchy but a democracy, erected on the belief that as the sons of God all men are equal. As to the economic system of Serenia, there is private ownership of goods, and some have more than others; but the weak are not exploited by the strong, and none are allowed to suffer through want. In his New Testament Melville marked verses in Acts describing what happened on the Day of Pentecost when Peter converted three thousand souls: "And all that believed were together, and had all things common; And sold their possessions and goods, and parted them to all men, as every man had need."[98] Thought of such a system may have been behind the statement that the social state of Serenia "is imperfect; and long must remain so." In Serenia man is not considered vile, as in Maramma; nor, on the other hand, is he believed to be capable of perfection. He is thought rather to have in his heart a germ of goodness which can be developed. The vicious are separated from the virtuous until they are reclaimed, but the treatment they are given soon remedies their defects.

In Serenia no reference is made to previous incarnations of Alma; his divinity makes him unique: ". . . never before was virtue so lifted up among us, that all might see; never before did rays from heaven descend to glorify it." But he is loved not only because he came from the Deity and performed miracles and gives life eternal, but also because of "an instinct in us;—a fond, filial, reverential feeling."

There are no temples in Serenia: "Alma preached in open fields,—and must his worshippers have palaces?" Money that might have been used for temples is used for charity. There is also no priesthood—a fact which emphasizes all Melville's criticisms of the clergy. Here all are apostles, living their religion every day in the week, and worshiping in a simple way. They do not fast. Their aspirations are their prayers. Instead of being long-faced, they consider laughter a means of praising God. As to the practicability of Alma's teachings, these were given for life on earth, not in heaven. In Serenia no man is persecuted because he disagrees with the majority: ". . . if he dissent from us, we then equally dissent from him; and men's faculties are Oro-given. Nor will we say that he is wrong, and we are right; for this we know not, absolutely."

The important thing here is not what a man professes but what he does. "He who hourly prays to Alma, but lives not up to the world-wide love and charity—that man is more an unbeliever than he who verbally rejects the Master, but does his bidding." In his New Testament Melville marked a number of verses having to do with faith and works, among them two which aptly express the attitude maintained in Serenia: "What doth it profit, my brethren, though a man say he hath faith, and have not works? can faith save him?" And: "Yea, a man may say, Thou hast faith, and I have works, and I will shew thee my faith by my works."[99] Alma is the supreme example of man doing good works: "He fed the famishing; he healed the sick; he bound up wounds. For every precept that he spoke he did ten thousand mercies."

No peculiar revelation was made by Alma. "All that is vital in the Master's faith, lived here in Mardi and in humble dells, was practised long previous to the Master's coming." In this connection one thinks of the praise that Melville bestowed on Seneca as an anonymous pagan moralist. Perhaps relevant also is Melville's marking years later in Arnold's *Literature and Dogma* a passage on a critic who maintained that the more one studies, the more one is convinced "that the religion which calls itself revealed contains, in the way of what is good, nothing which is not the incoherent and ill-digested residue of the wisdom of the ancients."[100] Certainly in the section on Serenia, Melville is concerned with presenting not the mysteries of the Christian religion but Christ's embodiment and glorification of age-old virtues, and especially his active sympathy for the unfortunate.

The religion of Serenia is said to contain nothing that conflicts with reason. "Right reason, and Alma, are the same; else Alma, not reason, would we reject. The Master's great command is Love; and here do all things wise, and all things good, unite. Love is all in all. The more we love, the more we know; and so reversed." Babbalanja, now converted from his speculative reasoning to right reason, says: "I have been mad. Some things there are we must not think of. . . . Reason no longer domineers; but still doth speak."

The only traveler not converted is Taji, who as a symbol of Melville's rational appetite will be discussed later. It is sufficient to say here that at the time of writing *Mardi* Melville was too much concerned with metaphysical problems to subdue his reason. His interest in the nature of the Deity, the question of man's immortality, and other such subjects was to assert itself in various ways in the future. But in his next two books he was to devote himself especially to advocating some of the values set forth in his account of Serenia.

CHAPTER III

LAY PREACHER AND FRIEND OF HAWTHORNE

NEITHER *Redburn* (1849) nor *White-Jacket* (1850) is so important an intellectual document as *Mardi*. The generally poor reception of the ambitious *Mardi* and Melville's increasing domestic expenses—he was already in debt[1]—made him try to regain favor with the public by returning to the simplicity of *Typee* and *Omoo*. His writing both *Redburn* and *White-Jacket* in a relatively short time,[2] his catering to the public taste in both narratives, and his private opinion that *Redburn* was "trash" should be kept in mind by anyone using these books as evidence of his thought.[3]

There is scarcely anything in *Redburn* and *White-Jacket* that expresses Melville's personal concern over theological problems. The references to God, immortality, and the like are very much in the conventional manner. Melville wrote these books not, as he wrote *Mardi*, for his own intellectual satisfaction, but in an effort to engage the attention of a Christian people. Yet in each work he has an exhortation to make that reveals a good deal about his religious idealism.

In *Mardi* Melville had shown his interest in Christian piety which manifests itself in deeds of kindness for the suffering. In *Redburn* he makes a plea for a widespread practice of such piety. He gets down to some of the fundamentals of social organization which he presented in his description of life on the isle of Serenia. He compares civilization to a coach, on which the lower classes of people are represented by the wheels: that those inside the coach may ride comfortably, the wheels must revolve in dirt and mud. Sailors, whose case he especially pleads, cannot be raised from their low estate in the social system until revolutionary changes have been made.

Though old seventy-fours and old frigates are converted into chapels, and launched into the docks; though the *Boatswain's Mate* and other clever religious tracts in the nautical dialect are distributed among them; though the clergymen harangue them from the pier-heads, and the chaplains in the Navy read sermons to them on the gundeck; though evangelical boarding-houses are provided for them; though the parsimony of shipowners has seconded the really sincere and pious efforts of Temperance Societies, to take away from seamen their old rations of grog while at sea:—notwithstanding all these things, and many more, the relative condition of the great bulk of sailors to the rest of mankind seems to remain pretty much where it was a century ago.[4]

In arguing for a more charitable attitude toward the unfortunate, Melville addresses his Christian readers in their own terms. Though in *Mardi* he had expressed much doubt about man's immortality, he asks in *Redburn:* "We talk of the Turks, and abhor the cannibals; but may not some of *them* go to heaven before some of *us?*" Not until we have learned "that one grief outweighs ten thousand joys will we become what Christianity is striving to make us."[5] A strong plea concludes the graphic account of the beggar woman and her three children whom he represents as being allowed to starve in the slums of Liverpool:

Ah! what are our creeds, and how do we hope to be saved? Tell me, oh Bible, that story of Lazarus again, that I may find comfort in my heart for the poor and forlorn. Surrounded as we are by the wants and woes of our fellow men, and yet given to follow our own pleasures, regardless of their pains, are we not like people sitting up with a corpse, and making merry in the house of the dead?[6]

In view of what Melville had written earlier, his admonitions to the clergy in *Redburn* are not surprising. The true profession of the clergy, he argues, is to save men from their vices. For that reason he greatly admires the chaplains who preach in the floating chapels and on the docks, exhorting the sailors in the simplest terms to give up "the two great vices to which sailors are most addicted, and which they practise to the ruin of both body and soul. . . ." In holding up these ministers as an example for the whole Christian clergy, Melville repeats the condemnation made in *Mardi* of idle worship of God in palatial halls:

Is not this as it ought to be? Since the true calling of the reverend clergy is like their divine Master's;—not to bring the righteous, but sinners to repentance. Did some of them leave the converted and comfortable congregations, before whom they have ministered year after year, and plunge at once, like St. Paul into the infected centres and hearts of vice: *then* indeed, would they find a strong enemy to cope with; and a victory gained over *him* would entitle them to a conqueror's wreath. Better to save one sinner from an obvious vice that is destroying him, than to indoctrinate ten thousand saints. And as from every corner, in Catholic towns, the shrines of Holy Mary and the Child Jesus perpetually remind the commonest wayfarer of his heaven; even so should Protestant pulpits be founded in the marketplaces, and at street corners, where the men of God might be heard by all of His children.[7]

In *White-Jacket* Melville answered the call he had made in *Redburn* for attacks on vice. Based partly on his experience aboard the frigate *United States,* this narrative records and condemns such evils on a man-of-war as drunkenness, gambling, sodomy, and particularly flogging.[8] Yet in view of the effectiveness sometimes attributed to the book as propaganda, it is well to remember what Hetherington said of *White-Jacket* in his dissertation on Melville's reputation: "Rather than originating the movement for reform in the navy, it rode the crest of the wave of an agitation which was already directed against flogging, and contributed somewhat, no doubt, to the final victory."[9]

The "general social condition" on these "Floating Hells," Melville affirms, "is the precise reverse of what any Christian could desire";[10] still on board each is a chaplain, who holds prayer twice daily with the men and preaches a sermon to them every Sunday. The Reverend Theodore Bartow, chaplain on the *United States* while Melville was aboard, was like the chaplain of the *Neversink,* the frigate of *White-Jacket,* in that he was Episcopalian;[11] but without documentary evidence it would not do to say that in *White-Jacket* Melville drew a portrait of Bartow. The chaplain of Melville's satirical portrait is genial, well-bred, and learned in Plato and the German philosophers, but he preaches sermons wholly unsuited to the crew. He stands in ridiculous contrast to the seamen's chaplains praised in *Redburn:*

Fancy, now, this transcendental divine standing behind a gun-carriage on the main-deck, and addressing five hundred salt-sea sinners upon the psychological phenomena of the soul, and the ontological necessity of every sailor's saving it at all hazards. He enlarged upon the follies of the ancient philosophers; learnedly alluded to the *Phaedo* of Plato; exposed the follies of Simplicius's *Commentary on Aristotle's "De Coelo,"* by arraying against that clever pagan author the admired tract of Tertullian—*De Praescriptionibus Haereticorum*—and concluded by a Sanscrit invocation. He was particularly hard upon the Gnostics and Marcionites of the second century of the Christian era; but he never, in the remotest manner, attacked the everyday vices of the nineteenth century, as eminently illustrated in our man-of-war world. Concerning drunkenness, fighting, flogging, and oppression—things expressly or impliedly prohibited by Christianity—he never said aught. But the most mighty commodore and captain sat before him; and in general, if in a monarchy, the state form the audience of the church, little evangelical piety will be preached. Hence, the harmless, noncommittal abstrusities of our chaplain were not to be wondered at.[12]

The motive for having chaplains in the navy is undoubtedly commendable, Melville says, but it does not follow "that, under the present system, they achieve much good, or that, under any other, they ever will." He inquires: "How can it be expected that the religion of peace should flourish in an oaken castle of war? How can it be expected that the clergyman, whose pulpit is a forty-two-pounder, should convert sinners to a faith that enjoins them to turn the right cheek when the left is smitten?" Pointing out that a part of the bounty paid for sinking an enemy's ship "full of human beings" is allotted to the chaplain, Melville asks the damning question: "How is it to be expected that a clergyman, thus provided for, should prove efficacious in enlarging upon the criminality of Judas, who, for thirty pieces of silver, betrayed his Master?"[13]   At the end of his life Melville in *Billy Budd* said as a final word on the subject:

Bluntly put, a chaplain is the minister of the Prince of Peace serving in the host of the God of War—Mars. As such, he is as incongruous as a musket would be on the altar at Christmas. Why, then, is he there? Because he indirectly subserves the purpose attested by the cannon; because, too, he lends the sanction of the religion of the meek to that which practically is the abrogation of everything but force.[14]

In *Deck and Port*, which appeared the same year as *White-Jacket*, the Congregationalist Reverend Walter Colton gave a different view of the life and activities of a chaplain in the navy. Yet, though he condemned the issuance of grog and believed in preaching simple, direct sermons to the sailors about their vices, he accepted flogging for want of a better substitute, and considered it glorious to fight for one's country.[15]

Colton's opinion that sailors made very poor Christians[16] was in agreement with Melville's contention that the sailors received little benefit from the religious services. They were compelled to attend the services whether they cared to or not, and sometimes they had to be driven by their superiors, who commanded them: "Go to prayers, d—n you!" They sat on uncomfortable seats made of "gun-rammers and capstan-bars, placed horizontally upon shot-boxes."[17] At the morning and evening prayer services many of the sailors were stationed where they could not hear a word of the prayers.[18]

This criticism of the religious exercises on a man-of-war is part of Melville's attempt to make his readers understand that if they put into practice the Christian principles they profess to embrace, they could do much toward abolishing the evils of civilization. He practically assumes the role of a preacher. Though he had recently expressed doubt about certain Christian doctrines, he here adapts Christian terminology to his own purpose, pleading with orthodox Christians as though their beliefs were his own. He had used this technique in *Redburn;* here he uses it to a much greater extent.

He addresses his readers as "fellow-Christians." He begs the attention of "Presidents of Peace Societies and Superintendents of Sabbath Schools."[19] He refers to Christ as "my Savior," "the divine Prince of Peace," "our blessed Redeemer," "He on whom we believe."[20] Despite his ridicule of the doctrine in *Mardi,* he makes it appear that he believes in the resurrection of the body. Of the flogged sailor he says: "And with these marks on his back, this image of his Creator must rise at the last day."[21] Representing himself as almost being flogged, he declares that he "meant to drag Captain Claret from this earthly tribunal of his to that of Jehovah, and let him decide between us."[22] In the name of their divine destiny Melville invokes the people of his nation. "We Americans are the peculiar, chosen people —the Israel of our time," he declares. "God has predestinated, mankind expects, great things from our race; and great things we feel in our souls." Striking a deeper religious note, he exclaims: "Long enough have we been sceptics with regard to ourselves, and doubted whether, indeed, the political Messiah had come. But he has come in *us,* if we would but give utterance to his promptings."[23]

The message of *White-Jacket,* however, is directed not only to the United States but to all Christendom, for the

Articles of War which it attacks are "an index to the true condition of the present civilization of the world." Melville sarcastically comments on "the pure, bubbling milk of human kindness, and Christian charity, and forgiveness of injuries which pervade this charming document, so thoroughly imbued, as a Christian code, with the benignant spirit of the Sermon on the Mount."[24] So long as the Articles of War are in effect, evil will prevail; "the whole matter of war is a thing that smites common sense and Christianity in the face. . . ."[25] By making men say that God directs them to victory, "war almost makes blasphemers of the best of men. . . ."[26]

In his despair Melville on one occasion laments: "Ah! the best righteousness of our man-of-war world seems but an unrealized ideal, after all; and those maxims which, in the hope of bringing about a millennium, we busily teach to the heathen, we Christians ourselves disregard." Then he hints at the subtle problem which later, in *Pierre,* he was to discuss at great length:

In view of the whole present social framework of our world, so ill-adapted to the practical adoption of the meekness of Christianity, there seems almost some ground for the thought, that although our blessed Savior was full of the wisdom of heaven, yet His gospel seems lacking in the practical wisdom of earth— in a due appreciation of the necessities of nations at times demanding bloody massacres and wars; in a proper estimation of the value of rank, title, and money. But all this only the more crowns the divine consistency of Jesus; since Burnet and the best theologians demonstrate that his nature was not merely human—was not that of a mere man of the world.[27]

Still he hopefully insists that men can find salvation in themselves. The "worst of our evils we blindly inflict upon ourselves. . . ."[28] In "our own hearts, we mould the whole world's hereafters; and in our own hearts we fashion our own gods. . . . Ourselves are Fate."[29] Men must live by their highest ideals; and the ideal that will end all war is embraced in a saying of Christ that Melville marked in his New Testament: "But I say unto you, That ye resist not evil: but whosoever shall smite thee on thy right cheek, turn to him the other also."[30]   In earlier works Melville had urged mankind to follow the example of loving-kindness set by Christ, but he had not singled out this tenet of Christian ethics for special emphasis.   In *White-Jacket* he writes:

Say on, say on; but know you this, and lay it to heart, war-voting Bench of Bishops, that He on whom we believe *himself* has enjoined us to turn the left cheek if the right be smitten. Never mind what follows.   That passage you cannot expunge from the Bible; that passage is as binding upon us as any other; that passage embodies the soul and substance of the Christian faith; without it, Christianity were like any other faith.   And that passage will yet, by the blessing of God, turn the world.[31]

The epilogue of *White-Jacket* sums up the state and the prospect of "our man-of-war world."   Melville takes into account present evils, but he expresses the optimistic faith that finally all will be well.   "God was the shipwright" and is the "Lord High Admiral" of our craft.   Though we "sail with sealed orders, and our last destination remains a secret to ourselves and our officers; yet our final haven was predestinated ere we slipped from the stocks at Creation." After brief moralizing in regard to the disheartening aspect of things, Melville ends: "Our Lord High Admiral will yet interpose; and though long ages should elapse, and leave our wrongs unredressed, yet shipmates and world-mates! let us never forget, that

'Whoever afflict us, whatever surround,
Life is a voyage that's homeward bound!' "[32]

Although this conclusion may make it appear that at the time of writing *White-Jacket* Melville was reassured by a definite faith in the benevolence of God and his purpose in creating the universe, there is also evidence in the narrative that he harbored some doubt.   Earlier in the book there is a passage which expresses the thought of the couplet with less assurance;[33] and in the epilogue itself there is a statement that should put one on guard against the dogmatic optimism of the couplet. "But let us not give ear to the superstitious, gun-deck gossip about whither we may be gliding, for, as yet, not a soul on board of us knows—not even the commodore himself; assuredly not the chaplain; even our professor's scientific surmisings are vain. On that point, the smallest cabin-boy is as wise as the captain."[34] This profession of skepticism alone causes one to wonder how Melville could confidently and sincerely go on to declare immediately afterwards that "Life is a voyage that's homeward bound!"

Full of doubt as *Mardi* reveals Melville to have been at the time of writing that book, there are instances of optimistic faith there, such as the passage which declares that we all shall join hands in heaven.[35] And in *Redburn*, after a lamentation over the condition of sailors, one reads: ". . . yet we feel and we know that God is the true Father of all, and that none of His children are without the pale of His care."[36] These lines and the closing lines of *White-Jacket* were motivated by kindred impulses.

There is reason to believe that during the period in which *White-Jacket* was written Melville had doubts as to the benevolence of the Deity identical with those expressed in *Mardi*, where it is asked why God creates men to suffer and die.[37] He refers in *White-Jacket* to a sin that "seemed something imposed, and not voluntarily sought; some sin growing out of the heartless predestination of things; some sin under which the sinner sank in sinless woe."[38] Writing of Bland, the villainous master-at-arms, he says: ". . . a studied observation of Bland convinced me that he was an organic and irreclaimable scoundrel, who did wicked deeds as the cattle browze the herbage, because wicked deeds seemed the legitimate operation of his whole infernal organization. Phrenologically, he was without a soul." Bland's depravity makes Melville ask: ". . . who is to blame in this matter?"[39]   Melville refuses to give a judgment, but one can deduce his answer to the question from what he says about a more merciful treatment of sailors who lose their courage under gunfire: ". . . it seems but flying in the face of Him who made such a seaman what he constitutionally was, to sew *coward* upon his back. . . ."[40]   The God-consciousness resulting from Melville's early Calvinistic training manifested itself in unorthodox ways.   In addition to the passages cited, there are some expressing such levity toward religious matters[41] as to bring Melville a rebuke from the *Southern Literary Messenger;*[42] and the reviewer for the *Literary World*, edited by Melville's Episcopalian friends Evert and George Duyckinck, was inspired by the book to warn Melville against undervaluing the forms of spiritual things "lest he get into a bewildering, barren, and void scepticism."[43]   Yet such criticisms are exceptions.   As Hetherington notes, the generally orthodox Christian tone was partly responsible for the popularity of the book among the people at large.[44]

The student of Melville's religious thought is confronted with a subtle problem when he considers that *White-Jacket* gives to a cursory reader the impression that its author was a fundamentalist Christian.   If at this time Melville believed in Christ as his redeemer, as various passages might be interpreted to show, he had a much stronger conviction of the doctrinal truth of Christianity than he gave evidence of in *Mardi*, published the year before.   If as an unbeliever he used evangelical terms only to gain the favor of his orthodox public, he was not so honorable a man as all the biographical evidence testifies he was.

The truth of the matter, however, appears to be that in *White-Jacket* Melville frankly assumed the role of the Christian reformer; for, with all its artistic excellence, the book is somewhat propagandist.   By the adaptation of Christian phraseology he made his appeal immensely more effective. Though he did not accept the teachings of Christianity in their literalness, he was a sincere believer in the truth and the virtue of Christian ideals. Justice, democracy, sacrifice, brotherly love, he was convinced, would save the world if the world could be saved. A fatalistic pessimism may sometimes appear in *White-Jacket*, but the book as a whole advances the sound, optimistic argument that men can overcome much evil if they but try. The problem as to why Melville wrote *White-Jacket* just as he did must apparently remain unsolvable. The fact remains that in its message of charity the book is true to Melville's highest ideals.

At the same time that he was expressing his Christian sympathies, Melville associated himself intellectually with a tradition of freethought. His mental attitude during this period is implied, for example, in his reference in *Redburn* to Hume as one who, though "not a Christian in theory, yet . . . died the death of the Christian—humble, composed, without bravado; and though the most sceptical of philosophical sceptics, yet full of that firm, creedless faith that embraces the spheres."[45] And it is explicitly shown in his determination, in the spring of 1849, to become acquainted at first hand with the views of Pierre Bayle, who has been called "the father of modern incredulity."[46]

On April 5, 1849, Melville wrote from Boston to E. A. Duyckinck: "I bought a set of Bayle's Dictionary the other day, & on my return to New York intend to lay the great old folios side by side & go to sleep on them thro' the summer, with the Phaedon in one hand & Tom Brown in the other."[47] The fact that Melville knew enough about Bayle to desire and to buy his *Dictionary* convinces one that he must have read a good deal in the volumes. Although he may not have been so much inspired by the *Dictionary* as Voltaire, Bernard Mandeville, the Encyclopedists, and other eighteenth-century freethinkers had been, it is reasonable to think that he was influenced by its critical method and some of its ideas. If he read the article on Pyrrho, to whom he refers in *Mardi* and *Moby-Dick*,[48] he was very likely attracted by the philosophical attitude of that ancient skeptic, of whom Bayle says:

He found in all things reasons to affirm and to deny; and therefore he suspended his assent after he had well examined the arguments *pro* and *con*, and reduced all his conclusions to a *non liquet, let the matter be further inquired into*. Hence it is that he sought truth as long as he lived, but he so contrived the matter, as never to grant that he had found it.[49]

If he read the article on the Marcionites, whom he mentions in *White-Jacket*,[50] he must have been stimulated by the heretical ideas of those early rivals of Christianity. Cross references in this article would have led him to related articles, such as those on the Paulicians and the Manichees; and Bayle's discussions of these three sects are notable since in them Bayle tries to account for the evil in the universe. Here Melville may have become acquainted with the Gnostic theory that the Creator of the universe is an inferior Deity. Here he may have been impressed by the arguments that would prove the Christian God to be cruel. Other articles, for instance that on David, would have given him a startlingly new conception of certain scriptural heroes. In fact, Melville's buying a set of Bayle's *Dictionary* in the spring of 1849 may have resulted in more profound influences in the development of his religious thought than any ordinary literal evidence will reveal.

In the fall of 1849, when Melville made a voyage to England and the Continent, he kept a journal which discloses something of the complexity of his religious attitude at that time. Though he thought that money spent for the erection of costly churches might better have been used for charity, he admired church architecture,[51] and while abroad he visited many cathedrals and chapels. But it was more than an interest in architecture that made him attend church services. On only one of the seven Sundays he was in Europe did he fail to join some congregation for worship,

and sometimes he went to both morning and evening services. There is something pathetic in his account of how on
one weekday he "Walked to St. Paul's and sat over an hour
in a dozy state listening to the chanting of the choir. Felt
homesick and sentimentally unhappy."[52] He wrote more
in his usual tone when he recorded going to St. Thomas's
to hear his

famed namesake (almost) "The Reverend H. Melvill." I
had seen him placarded as to deliver a charity sermon. The
church was crowded—the sermon admirable (granting the Rev.
gentleman's premises). Indeed he deserves his reputation. I
do not think that I hardly ever heard so good a discourse before
—that is for an "orthodox" divine.[53]

The total impression of his remarks on visiting cathedrals
and attending services is that he had a vital interest in the
Christian religion.

Another side of his thought is shown by several entries
in the journal referring to some earnest conversations he
engaged in. His principal companions in such talks were
George J. Adler, lexicographer and professor of German in
New York University, and a Dr. Taylor who was a cousin
to Bayard Taylor; both of these men knew German philosophy well. In addition to what the following passage tells
about Adler, it reveals the kind of subjects that Melville
liked to discuss:

His philosophy is *Coleridgean;* he accepts the Scriptures as
divine, and yet leaves himself free to inquire into Nature. He
does not take it, that the Bible is absolutely infallible, and that
anything opposed to it in Science must be wrong. He believes
that there are things not of God and independent of Him,—
things that would have existed were there no God; such as that
two and two make four; for it is not that God so decrees mathe-
matically, but that in the very nature of things, the fact is thus.[54]

On several occasions during the voyage, and later when he
was with Adler in England and on the Continent, Melville
engaged in conversations on Swedenborg, Kant, Hegel,

Schlegel, LaPlace, on free will, fate, foreknowledge, and the like.

It was only a few months after his return from Europe that Melville met Hawthorne, whose friendship was to mean more to him spiritually than that of any other man of letters. In none of the New York group with whom he had been associated had Melville found a companion whose temperament and ideas on religious matters had appealed to him so much.

The literary friends in New York who did a great deal to bring Melville out socially and to cultivate his interest in various fields undoubtedly contributed to his religious development.[55] During the early part of Melville's career as an author, Evert A. Duyckinck listened attentively to Melville's grudges against missionaries, and talked with him about books by religious authors. Among the volumes that he lent Melville from his excellent library were such diverse items as the works of Sir Thomas Browne; the book of characters *The Holy State and the Profane State*, by Thomas Fuller; *Margaret*, a curious religious novel by the Unitarian minister Sylvester Judd; and several volumes of Carlyle. It is possible that Melville showered Duyckinck with "sailor metaphysics and jargon of things unknowable" in the forties as he did one night in 1856, but no record of such talk has been uncovered.[56] The biographical interest of George Duyckinck in various Anglican worthies gave him something in common with Melville.[57] But these two friends were hardly ideal companions for the discussion of some of Melville's doubts. Evert Duyckinck was a staunch Episcopalian who went regularly to church; Mansfield says that "often his diaries recorded two church services on Sunday and others during the week."[58] George was not only a good Episcopalian but also treasurer of the Sunday-School Union and Church Book Society. It is not surprising that the *Literary World*, edited by these brothers, warned Melville against the dangers of skepticism.[59] There is no evidence that any of the other New York friends were the kind to inspire Melville to continual and long discussion of his religious doubts. N. P. Willis might be mentioned for his occasional expression of bitterness at being excommunicated from the Park Street Church in Boston, but, to quote Beers, he "never became skeptical; was not, at any time, in fact, a thinker on such themes and subject to the speculative doubts which beset the thinker."[60]

On the other hand, there is ample evidence that Melville found Hawthorne a kindred spirit. Just after the two had met, Melville published an encomium of "Hawthorne and His Mosses" which revealed that in Hawthorne's stories Melville found touches arguing "such a depth of tenderness, such a boundless sympathy with all forms of being, such an omnipresent love, that we needs must say that this Hawthorne is here almost alone in his generation,—at least, in the artistic manifestation of these things." Beneath the surface of Hawthorne's stories Melville perceived a gloominess similar to his own. It is the "blackness in Hawthorne," he said, "that so fixes and fascinates me"—a blackness which derived its power from appealing to the reader's concern over human depravity. Melville's admiration was so unbounded that he did not scruple to compare Hawthorne with "Shakespeare and other masters of the great Art of Telling the Truth."[61]

The two men came to know each other intimately. Melville visited Hawthorne for four days the next month, and during the following year they were fairly close neighbors in the Berkshires. To Melville their friendship was one which brought two great hearts together: he saw in Hawthorne and himself two of those few men who formed "a chain of God's posts around the world."[62] The entry in Hawthorne's journal for August 1, 1851, suggests the nature of some of their conversations: "After supper, I put Julian to bed; and Melville and I had a talk about time and eternity, things of this world and the next, and books, and pub-

lishers, and all possible and impossible matters, that lasted
pretty deep into the night. . . ."[63] Some of Hawthorne's
recorded thoughts on such subjects as immortality, the injustice of man's existence, and the inexplicable evil of one
man and goodness of another[64] give one reason to believe
that at least in the beginning of their friendship he found
some pleasure in metaphysical sessions with Melville. As
for Hawthorne's capacity to sympathize with Melville's
attitude toward the church and toward the Scriptural revelation, Hawthorne had written in his journal in 1842: "I
find that my respect for clerical people, as such, and my faith
in the utility of their office, decreases daily. We certainly
do need a new revelation—a new system—for there seems
to be no life in the old one."[65]

Full of "Promethean fire" himself, to use Mrs. Hawthorne's phrase about him,[66] Melville thought that he de-
tected the same spirit in the sympathetic Hawthorne. In
his "secret" review of *The House of the Seven Gables*,
which formed a part of a letter to Hawthorne, Melville
wrote:

There is the grand truth about Nathaniel Hawthorne. He
says no! in thunder; but the Devil himself cannot make him
say *yes*. For all men who say *yes*, lie; and all men who say
no,—why, they are in the happy condition of judicious, unin-
cumbered travellers in Europe; they cross the frontiers into
Eternity with nothing but a carpet-bag,—that is to say, the Ego,
whereas those *yes*-gentry, they travel with heaps of baggage,
and damn them, they will never get through the Custom
House.[67]

Hawthorne was a man of few illusions, but he was not the
thundering type, like Melville. Yet it is not what Hawthorne was so much as what Melville thought he was that
is important for understanding Melville. As the dedication
of *Moby-Dick* to Hawthorne implies, the relationship between the two men was a significant factor in Melville's
life during the period when he wrote the novel.

CHAPTER IV

ACCUSER OF THE DEITY

IN HIS ESSAY on "Hawthorne and His Mosses," Melville said that "in this world of lies, Truth is forced to fly like a scared white doe in the woodlands; and only by cunning glimpses will she reveal herself, as in Shakespeare and other masters of the great Art of Telling the Truth,—even though it be covertly and by snatches."[1] The various interpretations of *Moby-Dick* testify to the difficulty of discovering the precise meaning of the novel from the cunning glimpses of truth it allows. There is, of course, general agreement on many truths in the book; but different degrees of emphasis on those and insights into previously unseen "significances" —whether Melville intended them for significances or not— have resulted in some strange divergences of opinion as to what the whole means. It seems likely from the very nature of the book that critics will continue being, to a certain extent, each his own allegorist. The interpretation given here, which agrees with a number of others in the importance it attributes to certain passages, confines itself to what seems significant for the understanding of Melville's religious spirit at the time he wrote the novel.

To come at once to the central problem, the meaning of the allegorical conflict between Ahab and Moby Dick, Melville says explicitly what Moby Dick symbolizes for Ahab. Ever since the combat in which the white whale bit off one of Ahab's legs,

Ahab had cherished a wild vindictiveness against the whale, all the more fell for that in his frantic morbidness he at last came to identify with him not only all his bodily woes, but all his intellectual and spiritual exasperations. The White Whale swam before him as the monomaniac incarnation of all those malicious agencies which some deep men feel eating in them, till they are left living on with half a heart and half a lung. That intangible malignity which has been from the beginning; to whose dominion even the modern Christians ascribe one-half of the worlds; which the ancient Ophites of the East reverenced in their statue devil;—Ahab did not fall down and worship it like them; but deliriously transferring its idea to the abhorred White Whale, he pitted himself, all mutilated, against it. All that most maddens and torments; all that stirs up the lees of things; all truth with malice in it; all that cracks the sinews and cakes the brain; all the subtle demonisms of life and thought; all evil, to crazy Ahab, were visibly personified, and made practically assailable in Moby-Dick. He piled upon the whale's white hump the sum of all the general rage and hate felt by his whole race from Adam down; and then, as if his chest had been a mortar, he burst his hot heart's shell upon it.[2]

The novel also plainly says that the assault on Moby Dick signifies more than a mere assault on evil. For evil is but an effect, and Ahab is interested in the primary cause. Reasoning by analogy, in the manner of divines arguing for God's beneficence, Ahab concludes that if good is to be attributed to the omnipotent Deity, so must evil. When gazing one day at a calm sea beneath "a smiling sky," he exclaims: "Look! see yon albicore! who put it into him to chase and fang that flying fish? Where do murderers go, man? Who's to doom, when the judge himself is dragged to the bar?"[3] For him the visible world is but the manifestation of the spiritual: ". . . not the smallest atom stirs or lives on matter, but has its cunning duplicate in mind."[4] When Ahab strikes at Moby Dick, the symbol of all spiritual as well as all physical evil, he does so in a mad desire for revenge on God, whom he holds responsible for its existence. Ahab explains this when he says to Starbuck:

All visible objects, man, are but as pasteboard masks. But in each event—in the living act, the undoubted deed—there, some unknown but still reasoning thing puts forth the mouldings of its features from behind the unreasoning mask. If man will strike, strike through the mask! How can the prisoner reach

outside except by thrusting through the wall? To me, the
White Whale is that wall, shoved near to me. Sometimes I
think there's naught beyond. But 'tis enough. He tasks me;
he heaps me; I see in him outrageous strength, with an inscrutable malice sinewing it. That inscrutable thing is chiefly
what I hate; and be the White Whale agent, or be the White
Whale principal, I will wreak that hate upon him.[5]

A contemporary French critic got at the heart of the matter
when he said that the only reason Ahab tries to harpoon
Moby Dick is that he cannot harpoon God.[6]

By various devices Melville makes the white whale an
imposing symbol of divine power. The crazy Shaker
prophet Gabriel pronounces Moby Dick to be "no less a
being than the Shaker God incarnated."[7] Although Moby
Dick is represented as an agent for the first cause rather
than as the first cause itself, to conceive of a god's being
incarnate in a whale is not unprecedented, as Melville was
aware. Twice in the novel he refers to the oriental myth
of "the incarnation of Vishnu in the form of leviathan."[8]
And he plays with the idea of a leviathan deity by asserting
that "If hereafter any highly cultured, poetical nation shall
lure back to their birth-right, the merry May-day gods of
old; and livingly enthrone them again in the now egotistical
sky; in the now unhaunted hill; then be sure, exalted to
Jove's high seat, the great sperm whale shall lord it."[9] He
suggestively compares the white whale with Jupiter incarnate in a white bull, and even refers to the whale as "the
grand god."[10]

Moby Dick is invested with "terrors unborrowed from
anything that visibly appears,"[11] and with some attributes
unmistakably divine. Haunted by the legends about him,[12]
superstitious sailors believe him to be both ubiquitous and
immortal. His intelligence is considered far superior to
mere animal instinct: ". . . such seemed the White Whale's
infernal aforethought of ferocity, that every dismembering
or death he caused, was not wholly regarded as having been

inflicted by an unintelligent agent."[13]   There is a supernatural awe in his whiteness, which "is at once the most meaning symbol of spiritual things, nay, the very veil of the Christian's Deity; and yet . . . the intensifying agent in things the most appalling to mankind."[14]   At the end of the novel, just after the whale with "retribution, swift vengeance, eternal malice" in his aspect has rammed the ship, Ahab cries that the hull is "god-bullied."[15]

To carry out his blasphemous plan, Ahab fittingly has a crew that the devil himself might have chosen.[16]   Fedallah is obviously a sort of Mephistopheles to Ahab.   The five Manilla oarsmen of Ahab's boat are hinted to be "paid spies and secret confidential agents on the water of the devil, their lord."[17]   Starbuck characterizes most of the men when he calls them "a heathen crew that have small touch of human mothers in them!   Whelped somewhere by the sharkish sea."[18]   The mates too abet Ahab's purpose: the crew is "morally enfeebled . . . by the incompetence of mere unaided virtue or rightmindedness in Starbuck, the invulnerable jollity of indifference and recklessness in Stubb, and the pervading mediocrity of Flask."[19]

Since Ahab's attitude toward the Deity is precisely the opposite of Christlike submissiveness, it is ironically appropriate that the *Pequod* sets sail on Christmas Day.   Ahab's incantation over the harpoon he tempers in savage blood is also in harmony with his defiance: "*Ego non baptizo te in nomine patris, sed in nomine diaboli.*"   The omission of reference to the Son and the Holy Ghost emphasizes the fact that Ahab's feud is with God alone.   As Ahab pursues the white whale, he continues venting his blasphemy, though in a veiled way.   Since Melville was depending for his livelihood on the sale of his books in a Christian land, and since, moreover, he had no perverted desire to offend good Christian people, he caused Ahab to address his insulting remarks to "the gods," "the heavens," "thou clear spirit," and the like.   What Ahab says makes it fitting that he should have been named after King Ahab of old, who, according to the Bible, "did more to provoke the Lord God of Israel to anger than all the kings of Israel that went before him."[20] (He is like the scriptural Ahab also in that a prophetic Elijah foretells his doom.)

In one of his outbursts against the gods Ahab metaphorically calls them by the names of two contemporary prizefighters who engaged in a famous bout, and then, in a different figure, goes on to call them cowards:

I laugh and hoot at ye, ye cricket-players, ye pugilists, ye deaf Burkes and blinded Bendigoes! I will not say as schoolboys do to bullies,—Take some one of your own size; don't pommel *me*! No, ye've knocked me down, and I am up again; but *ye* have run and hidden. Come forth from behind your cotton bags! I have no long gun to reach ye. Come, Ahab's compliments to ye; come and see if ye can swerve me.[21]

In another scene he calls the gods jacks-of-all-trades, and says that they are unprincipled. In the typhoon he becomes vulgar toward the Deity. "What a hooroosh aloft there!" he cries of the winds. "I would e'en take it for sublime, did I not know that the colic is a noisy malady. Oh, take medicine, take medicine!"[22]

Some of Ahab's more serious charges against the Deity are made in the chapter entitled "The Candles,"[23] which tells how during the storm the corposants appeared: "All the yard-arms were tipped with a pallid fire; and touched at each tri-pointed lightning-rod-end with three tapering white flames, each of the three tall masts was silently burning in that sulphurous air, like three gigantic wax tapers before an altar." The symbolism implies what Melville goes on explicitly to say: "God's burning finger has been laid on the ship." Using fire as a symbol for the Deity might have been suggested to him by knowledge of Zoroastrianism, Heraclitus, the Stoics, the Bible, or various other sources.

Instead of being awed by this "Mene, Mene, Tekel Upharsin," Ahab defiantly brings charges against the Deity.

One of them is suggestive of Gnostic influence. In primitive Christian times the Gnostics urged rebellion against the Creator of the universe. They taught that He is an emanation from a higher power, that He is ignorant of His genealogy, and that He tyrannically governs the world in the belief that He is the Supreme God.[24] That Melville was aware of these heretics is evident from his reference in *White-Jacket* to "the Gnostics and Marcionites of the second century of the Christian era"; he might have read of them in such works as Bayle's *Dictionary* and Tertullian's *De Praescriptionibus Haereticorum*.[25] There is a hint of Gnostic influence in a passage in one of Melville's letters to Hawthorne, written in 1851: "We incline to think that God cannot explain His own secrets, and that He would like a little information upon certain points Himself."[26] Ahab brings what seems to be a definitely Gnostic accusation against God when he says to the symbolical corposants:

Thou knowest not how came ye, hence callest thyself unbegotten; certainly knowest not thy beginning, hence callest thyself unbegun. I know that of me, which thou knowest not of thyself, oh, thou omnipotent. There is some unsuffusing thing beyond thee, thou clear spirit, to whom all thy eternity is but time, all thy creativeness mechanical. Through thee, thy flaming self, my scorched eyes do dimly see it. Oh, thou foundling fire, thou hermit immemorial, thou too hast thy incommunicable riddle, thy unparticipated grief.[27]

On another occasion Ahab expresses the suspicion that there is no first cause. Melville's reading of Spinoza or his disciples may have been responsible for this note. In a volume of Matthew Arnold which Melville read in later years, he marked the following quotation from Van Vloten: "But it is in his having done away with final causes, *and with God along with them*, that Spinoza's true merit consists."[28] And in his copy of James Thomson's *Essays and Phantasies* Melville drew a line beside these words quoted from Spinoza: ". . . all final causes are nothing but pure fic-

tions imagined by men."[29]   Together with references to
Spinoza in *Mardi*,[30] these markings give one reason to
assume that Melville had reflected upon ideas as Spinozistic
during his earlier career.   Possibly such reflection caused
him, in the letter to Hawthorne referred to just above, to
say in regard to the higher powers:

And perhaps, after all, there is *no* secret.   We incline to think
that the Problem of the Universe is like the Freemason's
mighty secret, so terrible to all children.   It turns out, at last,
to consist in a triangle, a mallet, and an apron,—nothing
more! . . .   But it is this *Being* of the matter; there lies the
knot with which we choke ourselves.   As soon as you say *Me,
a God, a Nature,* so soon you jump off from your stool and
hang from the beam.   Yes, that word is the hangman.   Take
God out of the dictionary, and you would have Him in the
street.[31]

In *Moby-Dick* there is an analogous expression of this idea
in Ahab's statement that he sometimes doubts there is anything beyond the universal forces which the White Whale
symbolizes: "Sometimes I think there's naught beyond."[32]
This idea, however, like that which smacks of Gnosticism,
remains undeveloped.   Considering his thought as a whole,
it seems safe to give much weight to the monotheism expressed when Ahab enforces his authority over that of Starbuck: "There is one God that is Lord over the earth, and
one captain that is lord over the *Pequod*."[33]

The most important comments that Ahab makes about
God are those which give the reason for his defiance.   By
way of preface to the following quotation, Ahab's being
burned in the act of worshiping fire, or God, on the high
seas may be clarified by recalling that Melville uses exploring the seas to represent looking for the highest truth and
that in *Pierre* he refers to fire as "an eloquent symbol" of
the "ultimate Truth itself"[34] (in *Moby-Dick* he says that
"clear truth is a thing for salamander giants only to en-
counter").[35]   Having fire symbolize both the Deity and the

ultimate truth is not strange when one recalls the theological notion that God not only is true but is the Truth.[36]   As to Ahab's burn, he is described on his first appearance in the novel as bearing a long white scar like that which lightning sometimes makes in the trunk of a lofty tree.[37]   In addressing the symbolical flames, Ahab says:

Oh! thou clear spirit of clear fire, whom on these seas I as Persian once did worship, till in the sacramental act so burned by thee, that to this hour I bear the scar; I now know thee, thou clear spirit, and I now know that thy right worship is defiance. To neither love nor reverence wilt thou be kind; and e'en for hate thou canst but kill; and all are killed. . . . But war is pain, and hate is woe. Come in thy lowest form of love, and I will kneel and kiss thee; but at thy highest, come as mere supernal power; and though thou launchest navies of full-freighted worlds, there's that in here that still remains indifferent.

Then he refers to the ancient idea that man is animated by the divine fire: "Oh, thou clear spirit, of thy fire thou madest me, and like a true child of fire, I breathe it back to thee."[38]

It is clear that Ahab conceives God to be without love for mankind. When Melville was completing *Moby-Dick*, he wrote to Hawthorne: "The reason the mass of men fear God, and *at bottom dislike* Him, is because they rather distrust His heart, and fancy Him all brain like a watch."[39] Ahab typifies this dislike of God for His heartlessness. Looking upon the misery of the insane black boy Pip, Ahab exclaims: "There can be no hearts above the snow-line. Oh, ye frozen heavens! look down here. Ye did beget this luckless child, and have abandoned him, ye creative libertines." He says that Pip shall henceforth live with him, and Pip, clasping his hand, declares that he will never let go; whereupon Ahab cries: "Lo! ye believers in gods all goodness, and in man all ill, lo you! see the omniscient gods oblivious of suffering man; and man, though idiotic, and knowing not what he does, yet full of the sweet things of love and gratitude."[40] Ahab's severity with his crew should not blind one to the fact that his pity for mankind motivates his hostility toward the Deity.

Ahab maintains that he is predestined to play the role that he plays. "This whole act's immutably decreed," he tells Starbuck. " 'Twas rehearsed by thee and me a billion years before this ocean rolled. Fool! I am the Fates' lieutenant; I act under orders."[41] But as such critics as Holt, Winters, and Thorp have said,[42] there is much significance in the passage which tells how on some nights horrible dreams, born of feverish thinking of the day, caused Ahab to spring wildly from his hammock:

For, at such times, crazy Ahab, the scheming, unappeasedly steadfast hunter of the White Whale; this Ahab that had gone to his hammock, was not the agent that so caused him to burst from it in horror again. The latter was the eternal, living principle or soul in him; and in sleep, being for the time dissociated from the characterising mind, which at other times employed it for its outer vehicle or agent, it spontaneously sought escape from the scorching contiguity of the frantic thing, of which, for the time, it was no longer an integral. But as the mind does not exist unless leagued with the soul, therefore it must have been that, in Ahab's case, yielding up all his thoughts and fancies to his one supreme purpose; that purpose, by its own sheer inveteracy of will, forced itself against gods and devils into a kind of self-assumed, independent being of its own. Nay, could grimly live and burn, while the common vitality to which it was conjoined, fled horror-stricken from the unbidden and unfathered birth. . . . God help thee, old man, thy thoughts have created a creature in thee; and he whose intense thinking thus makes him a Prometheus; a vulture feeds upon that heart forever; that vulture the very creature he creates.[43]

Though Melville makes it clear that Ahab is responsible for his doom, he also shows great admiration and sympathy for Ahab. Melville considered Hawthorne and himself men of great hearts and keen intellects. He represents Ahab as "a mighty pageant creature"—a man "with a glob-

ular brain and a ponderous heart."[44]   Some men do not have
souls, but Ahab has enough "to make up for all deficiencies
of that sort in other chaps";[45] to use his own bold figure,
though his body has but one leg his "soul's a centipede, that
moves upon a hundred legs."[46]   Possessed of keen perception, Ahab is unable to enjoy the common delights of men.[47]
His abnormal consciousness of the grief in the world has
made him "impatient of all misery in others that is not
mad."[48]   His capacity for suffering is described thus:

In an instant's compass, great hearts sometimes condense to one
deep pang, the sum total of those shallow pains kindly diffused
through feebler men's whole lives.   And so, such hearts, though
summary in each one suffering; still, if the gods decree it, in
their lifetime aggregate a whole age of woe, wholly made up
of instantaneous intensities; for even in their pointless centres,
those noble natures contain the entire circumferences of inferior
souls.[49]

Ahab, one might say, has taken upon himself the suffering of mankind.   In a way to remind one of Jesus Christ,
he is pictured as standing before his men "with a crucifixion
in his face; in all the nameless regal overbearing dignity of
some mighty woe."[50]   The "Iron Crown of Lombardy" that
he wears was made, as Geist observes, "of the nails used in
the Crucifixion."[51]   Ahab feels as though he "were Adam,
staggering beneath the piled centuries since Paradise."[52]
His attack on the evil symbolized by Moby Dick, together
with this arraignment of God for permitting evil, is madly
enacted in behalf of mankind.   At the head of thirty-six
foreigners, an "embassy of the human race," Anacharsis
Clootz in 1790 spoke before the French Assembly for the
rights of man.   Melville refers to Ahab's crew as an
"Anacharsis Clootz deputation from all the isles of the sea,
and all the ends of the earth, accompanying Old Ahab in the
Pequod to lay the world's grievances before that bar from
which not many of them ever come back."[53]   Most men,
like Stubb, laughingly refuse to think about the problem of

evil; or, if they do think about it, solve it, like Starbuck, by letting "faith oust fact."[54] If Ahab were not intellectually honest and courageous, if he were less affected by the suffering of mankind, he would not be the tragic figure he is. As it is, too much reflection on the problem of evil brings him to madness.

The problem before the student of Melville's religious thought is how much of Melville, if any, is projected in Ahab's attitude toward the Deity.

There can be no doubt that Melville had thought a great deal about the evil in the world. *Mardi, Redburn,* and *White-Jacket* showed his keen awareness of its existence. Aside from what he said in the allegory of the novel, in *Moby-Dick* he showed his continued awareness of evil by incidental references to "the hideous rot of life," "the millions of miles of deserts and of griefs beneath the moon," the "horrible vulturism of earth," "God's great, unflattering laureate, Nature,"[55] and the like. Ahab says of himself that he is so far gone "in the dark side of earth, that its other side, the theoretic bright one, seems but uncertain twilight" to him.[56] It was in *Moby-Dick* that Melville said "that mortal man who hath more of joy than sorrow in him, that mortal man cannot be true—not true, or undeveloped. With books the same. The truest of all men was the Man of Sorrows, and the truest of all books is Solomon's, and Ecclesiastes is the fine hammered steel of woe. 'All is vanity.' ALL."[57] In regard to books, one recalls some of the authors in whom Melville had recently shown much interest: Shakespeare, with his unsurpassed knowledge of evil in the human heart; Burton, whose *Anatomy of Melancholy* abounds in the folly and madness of men; Hume, whose philosophizing on religion takes full account of the evil in the universe; Bayle, with his Manichaeistic insistence on the evil principle; and Hawthorne, with his gloomy studies of sin.

Melville's reasoning to account for the presence of evil may also be compared to Ahab's. In *Mardi* he presented the argument that since God has infinite power, evil could not exist unless God willed it; and he questioned the benevolence of the Deity in creating man to suffer and to die.[58]

Like Ahab, Melville considered himself an independent being. Ahab says to the fire symbolizing the Deity:

No fearless fool now fronts thee. I own thy speechless, placeless power, but to the last gasp of my earthquake life will dispute its unconditional, unintegral mastery in me. In the midst of the personified impersonal, a personality stands here.[59]

This sounds very much like Melville, who, in a letter to Hawthorne, referred with admiration to the type of man who apprehends "the absolute condition of present things" and who "declares himself a sovereign nature (in himself) amid the powers of heaven, hell, and earth. He may perish; but so long as he exists he insists upon treating with all Powers upon an equal basis." Then a shift to the first person reveals that Melville thinks of himself as such a man: "If any of those other Powers choose to withhold certain secrets, let them; that does not impair my sovereignty in myself; that does not make me tributary."[60] In other words, though God's inscrutableness puzzles Melville, it does not awe him into bowing down. Ahab, of course, is not content to be merely independent: he comes to disaster by hurling himself against forces of the Deity. But when he sees that he is doomed, he does not cringe; he exclaims just before darting his harpoon: "Toward thee I roll, thou all-destroying but unconquering whale; to the last I grapple with thee; from hell's heart I stab at thee; for hate's sake I spit my last breath at thee."[61]

In connection with Ahab's showing defiance rather than Christlike humility toward God, Melville's own attitude toward Christ in *Moby-Dick* is worthy of note. Whereas in *White-Jacket*, published the year before, Christ is held up as a model for all men to imitate, in *Moby-Dick* Christ is barely mentioned, and the only very significant reference to Him is uncomplimentary. In a passage extolling the beauty of strength, Melville comments on the charm of the statue of Hercules, on Eckermann's description of Goethe's manly corpse, and on Michelangelo's portrayal of the physical power of God the Father; then he adds the sentence:

And whatever they may reveal of the divine love in the Son, the soft curled hermaphroditical Italian pictures, in which his idea has been most successfully embodied; these pictures, so destitute as they are of all brawniness, hint nothing of any power, but the mere negative, feminine one of submission and endurance, which on all hands it is conceded, form the peculiar practical virtues of his teachings.[62]

In a volume of Shelley's *Essays* which Melville read later in life, he marked the following passage: "Milton's Devil as a moral being is as far superior to his God, as one who perseveres in some purpose which he has conceived to be excellent in spite of adversity and torture, is to one who in the cold security of undoubted triumph inflicts the most horrible revenge upon his enemy. . . ."[63] These lines could apply to Ahab as well as to Milton's Satan. It is even possible that this character influenced the conception of Ahab, for Melville was quite familiar with *Paradise Lost*.[64] But Ahab in the ideal is a far nobler character than Satan. Satan is a supernatural being who, though heroic, works by guile to achieve a selfish end. The all-too-human Ahab openly pits himself against a symbol of the divine power because he conceives God to have unjustly afflicted man.

Melville does not try to refute Ahab's criticism of the Deity as hardhearted. He does not say that God is loving and merciful. On the contrary, *Moby-Dick* contains evidence apart from what Ahab says that Melville thought of God as not wholly benevolent. The rhetorical apostrophe to "the great democratic God" is notable of Melville's democracy rather than of his adoration for a benevolent Deity. On the same page he says that "at the undraped spectacle of a valour-ruined man" piety itself cannot "completely stifle her upbraidings against the permitting stars":[65] the thought behind the astrological figure is obvious.

It is not surprising that savage members of the *Pequod's* crew should evince disrespect for the Deity, as in Tashtego's assertion that gods and men are both "brawlers";[66] but one of Queequeg's remarks deserves mention. When Queequeg almost loses his hand between the teeth of a dead shark, he says: ". . . wedder Fejee god or Nantucket god, . . . de god wat made shark must be one dam Injun."[67] This remark— so shocking that it was omitted from the first English edition of the novel[68]—reminds one of Melville's saying in *Mardi* that the seraph and the shark "were made by the same hand."[69] One might expect the good Father Mapple, of the seamen's bethel, to represent the Deity as kind, but his God is the stern, severe God of the Old Testament,[70] known to man chiefly by his chastising. Melville makes what seems to be an oblique hit at the Christian conception of a benevolent Deity when he says that Queequeg cherished Yojo, his little idol, "with considerable esteem, as a rather good sort of god, who perhaps meant well enough upon the whole, but in all cases did not succeed in his benevolent designs."[71] In another instance Melville says that occasionally God seems to be a jester. There are times "when a man takes this whole universe for a vast practical joke," when all dangers and misfortunes "and death itself, seem to him only sly, good-natured hits, and jolly punches in the side bestowed by the unseen and unaccountable old joker."[72] This passage makes it clear why Melville later marked a reference by Heine to the "great Author of the universe" as "the Aristophanes of Heaven."[73]

In connection with Melville's irreverent comments on the Deity, what a neighbor of his in the Berkshires said about him just after *Moby-Dick* was published seems pertinent. In a letter to George Duyckinck, December 28, 1851, Mrs. Morewood told of recently having the Melville family and others as visitors:

Mr Herman was more quiet than usual—still he is a pleasant companion at all times and I like him very much—Mr Morewood now that he knows him better likes him the more—still he dislikes many of Mr Herman's opinions and religious views —It is a pity that Mr Melville so often in conversation uses irreverent language—he will not be popular in society here on that very account—but this will not trouble him—I think he cares very little as to what others may think of him or his books so long as they sell well—[74]

One wishes that she had been more specific in regard to his irreverence.

Something of the same spirit that appeared in *Moby-Dick* and that Mrs. Morewood referred to in Melville's conversation may also be found in *Pierre,* which Melville had already begun writing. There he refers to the Deity as "the Infinite Haughtiness."[75] There, in writing of "that all-controlling and all-permeating wonderfulness" which, "by the generality, is so significantly denominated The Finger of God," Melville continues: "But it is not merely the Finger, it is the whole outspread Hand of God; for doth not the Scripture intimate, that He holdeth all of us in the hollow of His hand?—a Hollow, truly!"[76] The capitalization here lends more irony to the passage when one recalls that Melville had recently asked Hawthorne whether he did not think "there is a slight dash of flunkeyism" in the usage of capitalizing the Deity.[77] His fancy plays with the idea of God's ubiquity by representing Pierre as thinking that "rail as all atheists will, there is a mysterious, inscrutable divineness in the world—a God—a Being positively present everywhere;—nay, he is now in this room; the air did part when I here sat down. I displaced the Spirit then —condensed it a little off from this spot."[78] Displacement of the Holy Ghost by a human rump is hardly the sort of humor that one finds in an author wholly reverent toward the Deity. The humor of *Pierre* contains a touch of the spirit which characterizes Lucian's jests about the ancient gods and Voltaire's about the Christian God.[79]

In *The Confidence-Man*, published five years later, one of the characters refers to the Deity as the "high-constable" and the "high rat-catcher"; and at the end of the novel there is a jest about Providence that reminds one of some of Swift's vulgar humor. An old man wants a life preserver to take to bed, but he has no idea what one looks like. The cosmopolitan, also ignorant on the subject, hands him "a brown stool with a curved tin compartment beneath," saying that he thinks this is a life preserver. He says that in case of a wreck he believes the old man can "have confidence in the stool for a special providence." The other replies, "Then good-night, good-night; and Providence have both of us in its good keeping." The cosmopolitan says, "Be sure it will," and then as they are leaving, "Pah! what a smell. . . ." [80]

But to come back to *Moby-Dick*, we have Melville's own testimony on the spirit in which he wrote the novel. During the final stages of work on it he declared in a letter to Hawthorne:

Shall I send you a fin of the *Whale* by way of a specimen mouthful? The tail is not yet cooked, though the hell-fire in which the whole book is broiled might not unreasonably have cooked it ere this. This is the book's motto (the secret one), *Ego non baptiso te in nomine*—but make out the rest yourself.[81]

We know from Ahab's incantation over his harpoon that the secret motto in full is: *"Ego non baptizo te in nomine patris, sed in nomine diaboli."*[82] In the letter Melville does not say that this is Ahab's motto; he says that it is the book's. And in a letter to Hawthorne just after *Moby-Dick* was published, Melville says: "I have written a wicked book, and feel spotless as the lamb."[83] He does not say a book with a wicked character in it; he says a wicked book. And of course it was a wicked book according to the Christian world in which Melville and Hawthorne lived. Melville's inability to account for evil had made him conclude that the Christian conception of a wholly benevolent Deity is wrong, and he had arrived at the point where he could give full artistic expression to his heretical view without suffering pangs of conscience. Considering how far he had come from his early orthodox position, and how also the everlasting yeas of Carlyle, Emerson, and a host of others were ringing in his ears, there was reason for him to feel somewhat self-conscious, even though he was writing to a friend whom he believed to be, like himself, a thunderer of no.[84]

CHAPTER V

CRITIC OF CHRISTIANITY

SINCE the publication of *Moby-Dick* left Melville still in debt,[1] and since his eyes had almost failed him as a result of overstrain,[2] the prudent thing for him to do next was to write hastily a simple narrative that would pay him well. But he could not do this.[3] He had said after writing *Redburn*, which he thought "trash," that he hoped never to "write such a book again";[4] and he had later told Hawthorne: "What I feel most moved to write, that is banned,— it will not pay. Yet, altogether, write the *other* way I cannot."[5]

Now, in *Pierre*, he wrote a book that he knew would be "banned." He was both too intelligent and well-read a man and had had too much experience as an author to think that the public would be pleased with the unusual style, the exaggerated characterization, the shockingly unconventional theme, and the mysterious nature of the book as a whole. In giving the public such a novel, he seems to have been motivated in part by the kind of perversely humorous impulse to be reckless that a man sometimes has when he is in desperate straits.[6] But whatever his motives, he put into the book a great deal of terrifying truth, and some of this bears on the Christian religion.

A common criticism of religious novels published in America during the first half of the nineteenth century is that they present essentially false pictures of life. Faith too consistently wins over infidelity. The unbelieving hero or heroine is converted in the end, and not only is assured of everlasting bliss in heaven, but also frequently comes into substantial rewards on earth.[7] John Neal grew especially hot about the earthly dividends paid out by the authors of religious novels to pious characters that undergo trial and suffering.[8] Melville himself touched on the matter in his review of Cooper's *The Sea Lions*, in 1849, where he said of the love story:

One of the subordinate parts of the book is the timely conversion of Roswell, the hero, from a too latitudinarian view of Christianity to a more orthodox, and hence a better belief. And as the reader will perceive, the moist, rosy hand of our Mary is the reward of his orthodoxy. Somewhat in the pleasant spirit of Mohametan, this; who rewards all the believers with a houri.[9]

In *Pierre*, Melville wrote more severe criticism of contemporary novels. He satirized reviewers who preferred novels that could be "unhesitatingly recommended . . . to the family circle," novels that were "blameless in morals, and harmless throughout," that had as their end "evangelical piety."[10] Like Pierre, he had read enough novels to be repulsed at "their false, inverted attempts at systematising eternally unsystematisable elements." He knew that "the countless tribes of common novels laboriously spin veils of mystery, only to complacently clear them up at last."

Now, in his own novel, he tries to show the "unravellable inscrutableness" of life. *Pierre* begins simply enough; then it reveals how the hero, in difficulty, "began to see mysteries interpierced with mysteries, and mysteries eluding mysteries; and began to see the mere imaginariness of the so-supposed solidest principle of human association." And it ends like those "profounder emanations of the human mind," such as Shakespeare's tragedies, "intended to illustrate all that can be humanly known of the human mind; these never unravel their own intricacies, and have no proper endings, but in imperfect, unanticipated, and disappointing sequels (as mutilated stumps), hurry to abrupt intermergings with the eternal tides of time and fate."[11]

In telling his story Melville makes a more bitter attack on Christianity than he had ever made before. He had expressed an unfavorable attitude toward various aspects of

Christianity in his earlier novels, as, for instance, in his charges against the missionaries in *Typee* and *Omoo* and his rebellion against the doctrine of a beneficent Deity in *Moby-Dick*; but in *Pierre* he indicts the principles of Christian ethics by telling in great detail how a high-minded youth brings disaster on himself and several others by trying to live by the ethical teachings of Christ.

In the beginning Pierre has no difficult moral problem. The innocent youth is represented with great irony as living in an ideal world. Having just published a novel embodying a defiant attitude toward God for creating such a wretched world, Melville sings a mock hymn of joy over the loveliness of this earth:

Oh, praised be the beauty of this earth; the beauty and the bloom, and the mirthfulness thereof! The first worlds made were winter worlds; the second made, were vernal worlds; the third, and last, and perfectest, was this summer world of ours. In the cold and nether spheres preachers preach of earth, as we of Paradise above. . . .

Oh, praised be the beauty of this earth; the beauty, and the bloom, and the mirthfulness thereof! . . . Hosannahs to this world! so beautiful itself, and the vestibule to more.

Love reclaims all the earth from evil: "All this Earth is Love's affianced; vainly the demon ·Principle howls to stay the banns." In defining this Love which rules the world, Melville's fancy creates a ridiculous conceit: "Love is both Creator's and Saviour's gospel to mankind; a volume bound in rose-leaves, clasped with violets, and by the beaks of hummingbirds printed with peach-juice on the leaves of lilies." There is no misery among men: "Would Love, which is omnipotent, have misery in his domain? Would the god of sunlight decree gloom? It is a flawless, speckless, fleckless, beautiful world throughout; joy now, and joy forever!"[12]

Pierre not only is prospective heir to a large estate in this delightful world but also is heir to a fine Christian tradition. His father, who had died when Pierre was a mere boy, had left behind him "a marked reputation as a gentleman and a Christian."[13]   Mrs. Glendinning had thought him flawless. For a time Pierre is idyllically happy with his mother and Lucy, the girl he expects to marry.

But his dream world is shattered by a letter from a mysterious girl named Isabel, who says that she is his outcast illegitimate sister. For Pierre "the before undistrusted moral beauty of the world is forever fled"; his "sacred father is no more a saint. . . ."[14]   Pierre immediately resolves to help Isabel. But he does not wish to destroy his mother's happy memory of his father; and he knows, moreover, that his mother is too proud ever to accept the illegitimate girl. Yet he does not impugn his mother's pride: "He too plainly saw, that not his mother had made his mother; but the Infinite Haughtiness had first fashioned her; and then the haughty world had further moulded her; nor had a haughty Ritual omitted to finish her."[15]

The fact that he can expect no moral aid from his minister is revealed to Pierre when the Reverend Mr. Falsgrave and Mrs. Glendinning talk of a bastard child that has been born to Delly and Ned, two servants on the family estate. The irony with which Melville portrays Falsgrave (falsegrave?), the only minister in the book, indicates his contempt for the spinelessness of the clergy in facing real moral problems. His irony is much more vitriolic here than in the portrait of the chaplain in *White-Jacket*. One recalls by contrast the admiration that Melville had expressed earlier for rugged ministers who plunged into the centers of vice to fight evil.[16]

When Falsgrave comes to breakfast at the Glendinnings' to talk over the affair of Delly, he is quite happy; for he is in the presence of the "benefactress, from whose purse, he could not help suspecting, came a great part of his salary." He knows that Mrs. Glendinning and Pierre are very fond of him, and indeed he merits their favor:

Nature had been royally bountiful to him in his person. In his happier moments, as the present, his face was radiant with a courtly, but mild benevolence; his person was nobly robust and dignified; while the remarkable smallness of his feet, and the almost infantile delicacy, and vivid whiteness and purity of his hands, strikingly contrasted with his fine girth and stature.

Although born the son of a poor farmer, by means of his scholastic pursuits and by the indulgence of his "taste for the choicest female society," Falsgrave had acquired manners and accomplishments to grace his figure.

Heaven had given him his fine, silver-keyed person for a flute to play on in this world; and he was nearly the perfect master of it. His graceful motions had the undulatoriness of melodious sounds. You almost thought you heard, not saw him. So much the wonderful, yet natural gentleman he seemed, that more than once Mrs. Glendinning had held him up to Pierre as a splendid example of the polishing and gentlemanizing influences of Christianity upon the mind and manners. . . .

The excellence of Falsgrave's mind and talents and "his refined affinity to all things beautiful, visible or invisible," are certified by his eloquence and by his various essays on art, literature, and nature. A man of "beaming excellent-heartedness," he intensely dislikes having to manifest "an absolute dissent from the honest convictions of any persons, whom he both socially and morally esteems." Christ counseled his Disciples to use the wisdom of the serpent and the gentleness of the dove. On the morning of his visit at the Glendinnings', Falsgrave befittingly wears a "cameo brooch, representing the allegorical union of the serpent and the dove."

When the conversation at breakfast turns to the servants' bastard child, Pierre expresses regret over the wretchedness of Delly and her baby, but Mrs. Glendinning says that the "mother deserves it," and in regard to the child she inquires of the minister: ". . . what are the words of the Bible?" "The sins of the father shall be visited upon the children to the third generation," somewhat reluctantly replies the reverend man, quoting a Commandment the unjust ethics of which Melville had alluded to in *Moby-Dick*.[17]

Reflecting on his resolution to help Isabel, Pierre asks: "Should the legitimate child shun the illegitimate, when one father is father to both?" His mother answers emphatically in the affirmative; so Pierre puts the question more pointedly to Falsgrave: ". . . should the one refuse his highest sympathy and perfect love for the other, especially if that other be deserted by all the rest of the world? What think you would have been our blessed Savior's thoughts on such a matter? And what was that he so mildly said to the adulteress?" (In his New Testament Melville marked Christ's words of forgiveness to the adulteress; and he owned a print that portrays the scene.) Falsgrave's cowardice is shown in his evasive answer:

It is one of the social disadvantages which we of the pulpit labor under, that we are supposed to know more of the moral obligations of humanity than other people. And it is a still more serious disadvantage to the world, that our unconsidered, conversational opinions on the most complex problems of ethics, are too apt to be considered authoritative, as indirectly proceeding from the church itself. Now, nothing can be more erroneous than such notions; and nothing so embarrasses me, and deprives me of that entire serenity, which is indispensable to the delivery of a careful opinion on moral subjects, than when sudden questions of this sort are put to me in company. Pardon this long preamble, for I have little more to say. It is not every question, however direct, Mr. Glendinning, which can be conscientiously answered with a yes or no. Millions of circumstances modify all moral questions; so that though conscience may possibly dictate freely in any known special case; yet, by one universal maxim, to embrace all moral contingencies,—this is not only impossible, but the attempt, to me, seems foolish.

Pierre then inquires whether the biblical injunction, "Honor thy father and mother," should not always be obeyed; for, he says, ". . . as that command is justly said to be the only one with a promise, so it seems to be without any contingency in the application." He brings the question home: "For instance should I honor my father, if I knew him to be a seducer?" Mrs. Glendinning is horrified at the thought. The clergyman says: ". . . that is another question in morals absolutely incapable of a definite answer, which shall be universally applicable." Pierre excuses himself and quits the room.[18] Later, however, when he learns that Falsgrave has acquiesced in Delly's being driven from her home, he condemns the whole clergy, saying: "But I do not blame thee; I think I begin to see how thy profession is unavoidably entangled by all fleshly alliances, and cannot move with godly freedom in a world of benefices."[19]

Despite the discouraging words of his mother and Falsgrave, Pierre feels himself "divinely dedicated" to aid his illegitimate sister, even at the cost of all earthly affiliations and advantages. He resolves to make an "unequalled renunciation" of himself.[20] Since he is determined to give Isabel his constant fraternal love and yet not to expose his father's guilt to his mother, Pierre decides to make the world think that by a secret marriage he has already become Isabel's husband.[21] His anticipated marriage to Lucy would thus be wrecked; but he is confronted by "this all-including query—Lucy or God?"[22] Melville points out in regard to Pierre's decision "that, in a transcendent degree, womanly beauty, and not womanly ugliness, invited him to champion the right." Had Isabel been ugly and crippled would he have sacrificed himself in her behalf? But Pierre is represented as being unaware of Isabel's beauty as a subconscious influence on him. Consciously, he acts upon the purest motive, as is revealed in his having a "Christ-like feeling."[23]

Unhappy consequences follow. His mother disowns him, and later dies of madness. In the city, where Pierre has taken Isabel and Delly, and where Lucy joins them, matters rapidly grow worse. Pierre commits incest, he murders a kinsman who insulted him, he curses God. In the last scene, which is laid in a prison cell, Lucy dies of shock at hearing that Pierre is Isabel's brother; and Pierre and Isabel commit suicide.

This is an elaboration of an idea which Melville explicitly sets forth in the body of the narrative. If Pierre had thoroughly comprehended and had acted in accord with the teachings of Plinlimmon's pamphlet, which he found at the outset of his journey to the city, he would have escaped disaster.[24]

Before presenting the pamphlet, Melville asserts that the secret for reconciling the world with the soul has never been found. Plato, Spinoza, Goethe, the New England transcendentalists, and others who claim to have found it, all are "impostors." They "pretend somehow to have got an answer" from God; but "how can a man get a Voice out of Silence." Melville says that the pamphlet seems to him "more the excellently illustrated re-statement of a problem, than the solution of the problem itself"; but since men generally accept such illustrations for solutions, what is here presented may temporarily benefit someone.

The argument of the pamphlet is based on the conceit that wisdom is dual, being divided into heavenly wisdom and earthly wisdom. Though he had presented it in a very different spirit, and had not developed it, he had made use of this idea in *White-Jacket*, published two years earlier.[25] In *Pierre* Melville turns the idea to peculiar use. Entitled "Chronometricals and Horologicals," Plinlimmon's pamphlet compares Christ, with his celestial wisdom, to a chronometer regulated by Greenwich time; and man, with his best terrestrial wisdom, to a horologe carrying the time of a certain locality—Chinese time, for instance. Just as no Chinaman would be so foolish as to live by Greenwich time —"going to bed at noon, say, when his neighbors would be sitting down to dinner"—so no sensible man tries to live according to heavenly standards. In his New Testament Melville drew a line by Paul's assertion that the wise man of this world needs to become a fool to enjoy the favor of God.[26]   The pamphlet notes that although "the earthly wisdom of man be heavenly folly to God; so also, conversely, is the heavenly wisdom of God an earthly folly to man."   Christ said: "My wisdom (time) is not of this world."   And "whatever is really peculiar in the wisdom of Christ seems precisely the same folly to-day as it did 1850 years ago."

This folly brings about more disastrous consequences than does ordinary folly.   In *Typee* Melville had criticized the missionaries by pointing out that the benevolence of their intentions did not necessarily mean that their endeavors resulted in good.   Their cause was "in truth a just and holy cause":

But if the great end proposed by it be spiritual, the agency employed to accomplish that end is purely earthly; and, although the object in view be the achievement of much good, that agency may nevertheless be productive of evil.   In short, missionary undertaking, however it may be blessed of Heaven, is in itself but human; and subject, like everything else, to errors and abuses.[27]

In *Pierre* Melville goes a step further in asserting the danger attendant upon man's being guided entirely by spiritual standards.   Although Christ, even in woe, was enabled by his divinity to remain wholly free of folly and sin, any ordinary mortal who tries to live strictly by heavenly ideals is apt to become involved "in strange, *unique* follies and sins, unimagined before."   The tragedy of Pierre of course illustrates the point.   What Pierre considers "the uttermost virtue" proves, after all, "but a betraying pander to the monstrousest vice."[28]

Whereas the ethics of Christ call upon one to sacrifice himself entirely for his fellow men, the pamphlet says that under no circumstances should one make such a sacrifice. The pamphlet echoes numerous writers on ethics in saying that both for his own good and for the public good man cannot afford to ignore his impulses toward self-gratification. Shaftesbury, whom Melville had mentioned in a recent letter to Hawthorne, argued thus, for instance, in his *Characteristics*.[29]   In arguing for "the middle way" between promoting one's own good and the social good, Bishop Butler, in the Preface to his sermons "Upon Human Nature," uses a comparison that makes one think of Plinlimmon's chronometer and horologe.   Butler says that "our nature, *i.e.* constitution, is adapted to virtue, as from the idea of a watch it appears, that its nature, *i.e.* constitution or system, is adapted to measure time."   Among the various "parts" which constitute man's nature are the desires for personal happiness; to a certain extent these must be gratified.[30]   Melville sets forth his views on the subject in a passage which is noteworthy not only for its realization of mortal limitations but also for its tolerance and broad theism:

. . . if a man gives with a certain self-considerate generosity to the poor; abstains from doing downright ill to any man; does his convenient best in a general way to do good to his whole race; takes watchful loving care of his wife and children, relatives, and friends; is perfectly tolerant to all other men's opinions, whatever they may be; is an honest dealer, an honest citizen, and all that; and more especially if he believes that there is a God for infidels, as well as for believers, and acts upon that belief; then, though such a man falls infinitely short of the chronometrical standard, though all his actions are entirely horologic;—yet such a man need never lastingly despond, because he is sometimes guilty of some minor offence:—hasty words, impulsively returning a blow, fits of domestic petulance, selfish enjoyment of a glass of wine while he knows there are those around him who lack a loaf of bread.   I say he need never lastingly despond on account of his perpetual liability to these things; because *not* to do them, and their like, would be to be an angel, a chronometer; whereas, he is a man and a horologe.

His reasoning brings him to the conclusion that a "virtuous expediency" is all that God expects of mankind in general.   Realization of this, he says, would do much good, especially if the Church desisted from its harmful indoctrination:

For, hitherto, being authoritatively taught by his dogmatical teachers that he must, while on earth, aim at heaven, and attain it, too, in all his earthly acts, on pain of eternal wrath; and finding by experience that this is utterly impossible; in his despair, he is too apt to run clean away into all manner of moral abandonment, self-deceit, and hypocrisy (cloaked, however, mostly under an aspect of the most respectable devotion); or else he openly runs, like a mad dog, into atheism.

Aiming at attainable ideals will put "an end to that fatal despair of becoming at all good," which often afflicts those who have tried to realize the unattainable.

As final proof for his thesis Melville turns to the history of Christianity. In view of his early training in Christian ideals and his earlier exhortations in the name of Christ, what he says here is very significant:

But if any man say, that such a doctrine as this I lay down is false, is impious; I would charitably refer that man to the history of Christendom for the last 1800 years; and ask him, whether, in spite of all the maxims of Christ, that history is not just as full of blood, violence, wrong, and iniquity of every kind, as any previous portion of the world's story? Therefore, it follows, that so far as practical results are concerned—regarded in a purely earthly light—the only great original moral doctrine of Christianity (*i.e.* the chronometrical gratuitous return of good for evil, as distinguished from the horological forgiveness of injuries taught by some of the Pagan philosophers), has been found (horologically) a false one; because after 1800 years' inculcation from tens of thousand of pulpits, it has proved entirely impracticable.

After this concise indictment of Christianity, Melville brings the fragmentary pamphlet to an abrupt end, stating that besides propounding "what the best mortal men do daily practise; and what all really wicked men are far removed from"; the lecture also offers "consolation to the earnest man, who, among all his human frailties, is still agonizingly conscious of the beauty of chronometrical excellence."

Melville himself was agonizingly conscious of the beauty of Christ's idealism. The Sermon on the Mount was to him "the greatest real miracle of all religions" because it shows Christ's vivid awareness of the evil in the world and expresses his "inexhaustible . . . tenderness and loving-kindness" for mankind.[31] Such works as *Mardi* and *White-Jacket* testify that the teachings of Christ were among the major influences on Melville's idealism.

But increasing disillusionment in the capacity of man to live by the peculiar ethical principles of Christ made Melville write a novel that he knew would displease the public. Besides denouncing the style, the characterization, and the plot of the book, reviewers called Melville immoral, irreligious, and even insane. The literary weekly edited by Melville's Episcopalian friends the Duyckincks said: "The most immoral *moral* of the story, if it has any moral at all, seems to be the impracticability of virtue."[32] Fitz-James O'Brien fairly well represented the contemporary attitude when he said that all Melville's books "have had their own share of success, and their own peculiar merits, always saving and excepting *Pierre*—wild, inflated, repulsive that it is."[33]

The fact that Melville wrote this book knowing that it would hurt his reputation is forceful evidence of his unhappy state at that time. By studying the novel more closely, one can see that here, as in *Mardi*, Melville presented in symbolical form what had happened to him spiritually.

CHAPTER VI

THE STORY IN THE SYMBOLISM OF
MARDI AND *PIERRE*

HERE, IN A LETTER of 1851 to Hawthorne, is the essence of the story that Melville partly told in the symbolism of *Mardi* and completely told in the symbolism of *Pierre*:

Until I was twenty-five, I had no development at all. From my twenty-fifth year I date my life. Three weeks have scarcely passed, at any time between then and now, that I have not unfolded within myself. But I feel that I am now come to the inmost leaf of the bulb, and that shortly the flower must fall to the mould.[1]

In the following discussion of this symbolism I am indebted especially to three men. E. L. Grant Watson revealed the meaning of some of the symbols in *Pierre*; then George C. Homans threw a good deal more light on Melville's dramatization of the life of his mind in both novels. Now Merton M. Sealts has done still more to clarify the hidden meaning of the narratives by discovering, from a lead in *Redburn*, the key to much of Melville's symbolism in Burton's *The Anatomy of Melancholy*.*

In *Redburn* there is a reference to "that theory of Paracelsus and Campanella, that every man has four souls within him. . . ."[2] Melville, as Sealts points out, had read

* Sealts's generosity in sharing his discovery with me for use here before publishing it in his own study of Melville's thought has put me very much in his debt. After Sealts had announced his discovery to me in a letter, I made use of it in evolving the views expressed here. Later, on reading his dissertation, I found certain discrepancies in our interpretations of the symbolism; but these discrepancies, of course, do not lessen my indebtedness for the lead he gave me. My indebtedness to Watson and Homans may be seen by comparing this chapter with Watson, "Melville's *Pierre*," *New England Quarterly*, III, 195-234 (April, 1930), and Homans, "The Dark Angel: The Tragedy of Herman Melville," *New England Quarterly*, V, 699-730 (Oct., 1932).

about this in the discussion of the soul in *The Anatomy of Melancholy*.³ Burton mentions only in passing that Paracelsus and Campanella add a fourth soul, "a spiritual soul," to the three souls, or three faculties of one soul, commonly referred to in the psychology of that time: the vegetal, the sensible, and the rational. Burton's own exposition of the soul is based on the three major divisions. The lower faculties, he says, can exist without the higher, but the higher cannot exist without the lower. The vegetal soul, the lowest, is "a substantial act of an organical body, by which it is nourished, augmented, and begets another like unto itself." The sensible soul, which also includes the vegetal, is an act "of an organical by which it lives, hath sense, appetite, judgment, breath, and motion." The rational soul, which includes both the vegetal and the sensible, consists of the understanding and the will. Melville uses certain features of this psychology in both novels: by having major characters symbolize various faculties of the soul, he relates the development of his inner life.

The setting in *Mardi* is appropriate for the enactment of such a story. Here land represents empirical truth and sailing the seas represents the search for truth by speculative or introspective reasoning. This symbolism, which appears in several of Melville's works, is explained in the passage in *Moby-Dick* which affirms that "all deep, earnest thinking is but the intrepid effort of the soul to keep the open independence of her sea," and that "in landlessness alone resides the highest truth, shoreless, indefinite as God. . . ."⁴

The greater part of *Mardi* tells about the voyage of the narrator, Taji, and his four companions throughout the islands of this strange world. The movements of these five characters symbolize the activity of certain faculties in Melville's mind. Burton divided the sensible soul into the outward part, made up of the five senses of seeing, feeling, hearing, tasting, and smelling, and the inward part, made up of the three senses of phantasy, memory, and common sense. Melville was not concerned with representing the outward part, but he did represent the inward part. King Media, as his name and his regal attitude toward the others indicate, symbolizes common sense; Yoomy, the young poet, symbolizes phantasy; and Mohi, the old historian, memory. The other two men represent the two parts of the rational soul: the understanding, "which is the rational power apprehending," and the will, "which is the rational power moving." Babbalanja, the philosopher, is a symbol of the understanding—"a power of the soul by which we perceive, know, remember, and judge as well singulars, as universals. . . ." Babbalanja significantly does by far the most talking. The will, represented by Taji, is the "rational appetite"; it has the power to choose between "such things as have been before judged and apprehended by the understanding." It is free to choose between what it conceives to be right and wrong. Two other important characters in the novel are Hautia, the dark woman, who symbolizes the vegetal soul, and Yillah, the fair, who symbolizes the spiritual soul. Though Burton says little about the theory of the spiritual soul, he does give the clue to the curious role played by Yillah: "Spirit is a most subtle vapour, which is expressed from the blood, and the instrument of the soul, to perform all his actions; a common tie or medium between the body and the soul, as some will have it; or as Paracelsus, a fourth soul of itself." Yillah is the first of these characters that Taji finds.

When Taji sails into the waters of Mardi, he is accompanied only by Jarl, an old seaman from the isle of Skye who has on his arm a tattooed image of the Crucifixion. Then he acquires another companion named Samoa, a native of the Navigator Islands. These two characters may be taken to reflect the northern Christian heritage and the South Sea pagan influence that were at work on Melville's will when his real development began.[5] These two are with Taji when he finds and rescues Yillah, who is about to be sacrificed. Immediately Taji is enamoured of the beautiful maiden.

In the relationship between Taji and Yillah, Melville represents the happiness that his rational appetite found in the spiritual soul. He was aware of the doctrine that the everlasting, the unchangeable truth is to be attained only through reason unhampered by the body. He might have found this doctrine in numerous sources. For instance, in Plato's *Phaedo*, with which Melville was familiar, one finds Socrates asking:

Must not, therefore, something of reality become manifest to the soul, in the energy of reasoning . . . ?—It must [says Simmias].—But the soul [says Socrates] then reasons in the most beautiful manner, when it is disturbed by nothing belonging to the body, neither by hearing, nor sight, nor pain, nor any pleasure, but subsists in the most eminent degree, itself by itself, bidding farewell to the body, and, as much as possible neither communicating nor being in contact with it, extends itself towards real being.[6]

St. Augustine, who is mentioned in *Mardi*,[7] is only one of many Church fathers who stressed the virtue of such contemplation. Yillah's divinity is indicated in her telling Taji just after he finds her that she is "more than mortal, a maiden from Oroolia"; Oro is the God of Mardi. Her being enraptured by Jarl's tattooed image of the crucified Christ[8] also hints of a celestial nature.

It is significant, as Sealts observes, that the page in *Redburn* referring to the doctrine of the four souls also mentions that "subtle power" of music which "enters, without knocking, into our inmost beings, and shows us all hidden things"; for Melville's symbolism reflects Plato's notion that music strongly moves the soul. The *Republic* asserts that "rhythm and harmony enter in the strongest manner into the inward part of the soul, and most powerfully affect it. . . ."[9] Yillah's affinity for music is suggested in her use of her shell, "one of those ever moaning of ocean," which is said also to have come from Oroolia: "Now, the maiden oft held it to her ear, and closing her eyes, listened and listened to its soft inner breathings, till visions were born of the sound, and her soul lay for hours in a trance of delight."[10]   When one recalls that Melville used land to symbolize empirical truth and sailing the ocean to symbolize introspective reasoning, there is a special significance in Taji's purposely turning away from the land to drift for several days with the newly won maiden he had found upon the sea.[11]   And later he does not settle with Yillah in a secluded spot on the mainland; he must have an islet just off shore.[12]   In connection with this symbolism of the sea, it should also be remembered that the infant Yillah's soul, enclosed in a blossom and borne by a shell, was fabled to have traversed these waters in coming from Oroolia.[13]

For a time Taji enjoys almost unbelievable happiness with Yillah.   He describes his feeling toward her just before she suddenly disappears: "Did I commune with a spirit? Often I thought that Paradise had overtaken me on earth, and that Yillah was verily an angel, and hence the mysteries that hallowed her."[14]   Yet, though he sees a celestial quality in her loveliness, he disbelieves from the beginning the mythology concerning her origin.   Since Yillah at first believes herself to be divine, and asks Taji whether he too is not divine, he induces her to think that he came from "her own fabulous Oroolia."[15]   Later, however, he tries to make her believe that what he told her about himself was revealed to him in dreams; and it is not long before he can contemplate "the extinguishment in her heart of the notion of her own spirituality."[16]

Melville suggests that what he at first conceived to be the spiritual soul derives from and is held in bondage by the vegetal soul.   One recalls Burton's statement that although Paracelsus considered the spirit "a fourth soul of itself," some considered it "a most subtile vapour, which is expressed from the blood, and the instrument of the soul, to perform all his actions; a common tie or medium between the body and the soul. . . ." The influence of such empirical philosophers as Hobbes, Locke, and Hume is also reflected in Melville's representation of the spiritual faculty as held captive by the body. Hume, whom Melville praised highly in *Redburn*, presented especially strong argument against the theory that there is anything spiritual about the reason.[17] After Yillah has disappeared and Taji has begun his long search for her, he learns that she is of earthly parentage, the daughter of beings white like himself, who had brought her to the islands as a baby. Then he exclaims: "Oh, Yillah! too late, too late have I learned what thou art!"[18] Her duality is suggested by the fact that when she once looked into the eyes of her bird and "saw strange faces there," she said: "These are two souls, not one."[19] When Taji rescues Yillah, she is about to be sacrificed by being plunged into "a vortex," a symbol which, as Homans notes, "looks phallic."[20] Though she escapes this fate temporarily, she feels that ultimately she will be drawn into the vortex.[21] Her relationship to the sensual woman Hautia, "the vortex that draws all in,"[22] is significant, since Hautia is a symbol of the vegetal soul. At the end of his voyage around the archipelago, Taji comes to the island of Hautia, who has sought from the beginning to tempt him. There he is led to conclude that in "some wild way, Hautia had made a captive of Yillah."[23]

The symbolical narrative reveals something about Melville's motives in devoting himself to introspective reasoning. When Taji finds Yillah, she is a prisoner of the priest Aleema, who has always kept her in seclusion and is now preparing to sacrifice her. Taji's preventing her from being plunged into the vortex symbolizes Melville's attempt to rescue the seemingly divine spirit from being sacrificed to the baser uses to which most men put it. But in the course of rescuing Yillah, Taji kills Aleema. This murder represents the will's violation of forces which would have prevented such extreme introspective reasoning as Melville indulged in.

The crime he has committed causes Taji to reflect on what incited him to the act:

Remorse smote me hard; and like lightning I asked myself, whether the death-deed I had done was sprung of a virtuous motive, the rescuing a captive from thrall; or whether beneath that pretence, I had engaged in this fatal affray for some other, and selfish purpose; the companionship of a beautiful maid. But throttling the thought, I swore to be gay. Am I not rescuing the maiden? Let them go down who withstand me.[24]

Soon afterwards he is more frank with himself. "Sifted out, my motives to this enterprise justified not the mad deed, which, in a moment of rage, I had done," he admits: "though, these motives had been covered with a gracious pretence; concealing myself from myself. But I beat down the thought."[25] After he has spent much time in search of Yillah, he makes the open confession: "The priest I slew, but to gain her, now lost; and I would slay again to bring her back."[26] Here one sees Melville admitting that the desire to please himself was at the bottom of his devotion to introspective reasoning, and that he repented of nothing he had done in order to indulge this tendency.

That following this course was not without painful consequences is symbolically portrayed in the pursuit of Taji by the furies, the three sons of Aleema who would avenge the murder of their father. They kill the two faithful companions, Jarl and Samoa, who had sailed with Taji into the seas where he found Yillah. At the end of the novel the avengers still pursue him.

Babbalanja, as a symbol of Melville's understanding, acknowledges the limits of human reason; he curbs his speculative tendencies and now, at the end, lives according to the "right reason" of Serenia—the reason which guides one in the wisest and purest moral living. He pleads:

Taji! for Yillah thou wilt hunt in vain; she is a phantom that but mocks thee; and while for her thou madly huntest, the sin thou didst cries out, and its avengers still will follow. But here they may not come: nor those [the syrens of Hautia], who, tempting, track thy path. Wise counsel take. Within our hearts is all we seek: though in that search many need a prompter. Him have I found in blessed Alma [Christ]. Then rove no more. Gain now, in flush of youth, that last wise thought, too often purchased, by a life of woe. Be wise: be wise.[27]

But Melville's will would not now be guided by his understanding. His rational appetite for the ultimate truth made him spurn the wisdom of humility. His pride and determination are shown in the autobiographical passage which says: ". . . if after all these fearful, fainting trances, the verdict be, the golden haven was not gained;—yet in bold quest thereof, better to sink in boundless deeps, than float on vulgar shoals; and give me, ye gods, an utter wreck, if wreck I do."[28]

As Babbalanja's counsel was without effect, so also, at the end, is Yoomy's warning: "Nay, Taji: commit not the last, last crime!" Taji turns the prow toward the outer ocean, saying, "Now, I am my own soul's emperor; and my first act is abdication! Hail! realm of shades!"[29] This "annihilation of the Ego," as Murray has called it,[30] represents the ultimate in the pursuit of reality. The last words of the book describe Taji as sailing "over an endless sea."

Three years later Melville told the story of his inner life again in the symbolism of *Pierre*. Meanwhile, he had continued his introspective reasoning, and now the story he had to tell was far gloomier. In his symbolism he makes use again of the psychology set forth by Burton, but here he is more artful: the drama is both more vivid and more tragic.

Pierre is a symbol of Melville's rational soul, which, one recalls, includes the will and the understanding in addition to the sensible and the vegetal souls. Taji was represented as a demigod in the world of Mardi. The explanation that Melville gives of Pierre's vision of Enceladus, to be discussed later, reveals that Pierre's father symbolizes the Deity and his mother symbolizes the world. In portraying his own early untroubled spiritual existence, Melville grows ironical. Pierre is ideally happy. A dutiful, loving son, he is smiled upon by his proud mother, just as Melville was at first smiled upon by the world. And just as the widowed mother tells Pierre that his father in heaven should be revered as the personification of virtue and goodness, so Melville's world admonished him to revere the Deity as perfect. Pierre worshiped his father with "the fulness of all young life's most reverential thoughts and beliefs."[31]

There are two portraits of Pierre's father.[32] One is a large handsome portrait which hangs conspicuously in Mrs. Glendinning's drawing room; she says this one is authentic. The other portrait, made before his mother's marriage and given to Pierre by his aunt, hangs in Pierre's own apartment. His mother thinks this portrait "namelessly unpleasant and repelling."[33] It portrays the father as ambiguously smiling and seeming to say: "Pierre, believe not the drawing-room painting; that is not thy father; or, at least, is not *all* of thy father. . . . Look again, I am thy father as he more truly was."[34] The attitudes of Pierre and his mother toward the portraits are significant as showing that in contradistinction to the conception of the Deity held by the Christian world at large Melville had a personal conception of the Deity which took into account certain curious puzzling features.

In *Mardi* Melville used young women to symbolize the spiritual and the vegetal souls; in *Pierre* he does likewise, and he adds a third to symbolize the sensible soul. The first of these to appear is Lucy, who represents the sensible soul. This faculty, as was said earlier, includes besides the vegetal soul common sense, memory, and phantasy together with the five ordinary senses and the power that causes all these to move; this faculty is that act "of an organical body by which it lives, hath sense, appetite, judgment, breath, and motion." Pierre has grown up with the healthy, lovely Lucy and is now engaged to marry her. His mother favors the match, because she knows that it will not interfere with her domination over her son. In this manner Melville represents his happy relations with the world during that early period when he cultivated his normal objective tendencies.

But Pierre's innocent happiness does not last. He receives a letter from Isabel saying that she is the outcast daughter of his father. This girl symbolizes the spiritual soul. The difference between the blonde Yillah and the ebony-haired sad Isabel is suggestive of the darker, deeper truth that Melville's exploration of the soul had revealed. Before Pierre received the letter from Isabel, he was haunted by her face, though he had seen it but once:

Nor had it accosted him in any privacy; or in any lonely byway; or beneath the white light of the crescent moon; but in a joyous chamber, bright with candles, and ringing with twoscore women's gayest voices. Out of the heart of mirthfulness, this shadow had come forth to him. Encircled by bandelets of light, it had still beamed upon him; vaguely historic and prophetic; backward, hinting of some irrevocable sin; forward, pointing to some inevitable ill. One of those faces, which now and then appear to man, and without one word of speech, still reveal glimpses of some fearful gospel. In natural guise, but lit by supernatural light; palpable to the senses, but inscrutable to the soul; in their perfectest impression on us, ever hovering between Tartarean misery and Paradisaic beauty; such faces, compounded so of hell and heaven, overthrow in us all foregone persuasions, and make us wondering children in this world again.[35]

For Pierre this face had uncovered "one infinite, dumb, beseeching countenance of mystery, underlying all the surfaces of visible time and space."[36]

It is significant that Pierre believes Isabel to be the daughter of his father, for as such she is divine. "That intense and indescribable longing" in Isabel's letter "was the unsuppressible and unmistakable cry of the godhead through her soul, commanding Pierre to fly to her, and do his highest and most glorious duty in the world."[37]   Pierre tells her that she is "made of that fine, unshared stuff of which God makes his seraphim."[38]   Burton says that spirit is "the instrument of the soul, to perform all his actions."   Isabel tells Pierre: "Thy hand is the caster's ladle, Pierre, which holds me entirely fluid.   Into thy forms and slightest moods of thought, thou pourest me; and I there solidify to that form, and take it on, and thenceforth wear it, till once more thou mouldest me anew."   Pierre replies, "The gods made thee of a holyday, when all the common world was done. . . ."[39]   On the night when she told him the second part of her story, with the heat-lightnings flashing outside, she "seemed to swim in an electric fluid," to be "moulded from fire and air,"[40] the two everlasting immaterial elements.

Isabel says that she "never knew a mortal mother"; her lips "never touched a woman's breast."[41]   In telling of her early life she symbolically narrates the growth of that part of the mind she represents.   In darkness and bewilderment she lived across the sea in a secluded forest hut with an uncommunicative old man and woman and a cat that hissed at her.   She dimly recollects crossing the sea, and then living for a time in a madhouse.   Even now she is mad sometimes.   Her wretchedness has not made her want happiness of an ordinary sort; there is something Buddhistic in her longing:

I pray for peace—for motionlessness—for the feeling of myself, as of some plant, absorbing life without seeking it, and existing without individual sensation.   I feel that there can be no perfect peace in individualness.   Therefore, I hope one day to feel myself drank up into the pervading spirit animating all things.   I feel that I am an exile here.[42]

Like Yillah's delight in her moaning sea shell, Isabel's enchantment by the murmuring sounds of her guitar reflects the Platonic idea that music speaks to the soul. Melville says that "where the deepest words end, there music begins with its supersensuous and all-confounding intimations."[43] But music is Isabel's own language. "All the wonders that are unimaginable and unspeakable," she says, "all these wonders are translated in the mysterious melodiousness of the guitar."[44] When the room is filled with "the infinite significances of the sounds of the guitar," Pierre tells Isabel to speak to him, "if thou indeed canst be a thing that's mortal." As she leans over the guitar, from beneath her flowing dark hair comes the words:

> Mystery! Mystery!
> Mystery of Isabel!
> Mystery! Mystery!
> Isabel and Mystery![45]

On one occasion she says: "Pierre, I am a poor girl, born in the midst of mystery, bred in mystery, and still surviving to mystery. So mysterious myself, the air and the earth are unutterable to me; no word have I to express them." When Pierre himself talks wildly, she continues: "Pierre, when thou just hovered on the verge, thou wert a riddle to me; but now, that thou art deep down in the gulf of the soul,—now, when thou wouldst be lunatic to wise men, perhaps—now doth poor ignorant Isabel begin to comprehend thee."[46] Melville's saying in *Moby-Dick* that "the highest truth" is "shoreless, indefinite as God"[47] is at one with Isabel's assertion that "better, a million times, and far sweeter are mysteries than surmises: though the mystery be unfathomable, it is still the unfathomableness of fulness; but the surmise, that is but shallow and unmeaning emptiness."[48] Surmises depend on particulars of experience; reality itself is mystery.

When Pierre finds Isabel, she is humbly serving Delly, who symbolizes the vegetal soul, the soul that generates and nourishes. It is Delly who bears an illegitimate child. When Pierre sets up his household in the city, it is Delly who waits on the others. She prepares the food and serves it in her room. The stove which heats the apartment is in her room; the stovepipe runs from this room through Isabel's, through Pierre's, and then outside. When Lucy joins the household, she occupies a room next to Delly's on the opposite side from the others; she receives heat by leaving the door open between her room and Delly's and by having a fire in her grate. Delly, of course, has a minor part in the story. Yet one should not overlook the significance of Isabel's being in attendance on Delly when Pierre finds Isabel, for thus Melville indicates that when he discovered his spiritual soul, it was doing humble service to the vegetal. One recalls Babbalanja's deploring that we should use our reason "but for a paw, to help us to our bodily needs, as the brutes use their instinct."[49]

In presenting the four souls in *Pierre,* Melville again makes use of the land to symbolize empirical truth and the sea abstract truth. Isabel, like Yillah, traversed the sea at an early age and came inland to the country.[50] Lucy has a home by the sea but has spent much time inland; she has two brothers in the navy.[51] Delly was born and bred inland. And, says Melville, it was *"the choice fate of Pierre to have been born and bred in the country."*[52] Life is infinitely harder for Pierre during the latter half of the novel, in which the scene is a seaport.

The discovery of Isabel brings about a great change in Pierre's life. He knows that his mother will not recognize Isabel, and he finds that he can get no moral support from the Church in aiding the outcast girl; but he is not to be deterred. Though it requires giving up the future he has planned with Lucy, he announces that he is married to Isabel so that he can be near her to give her the care and affection so long denied her. This step causes his mother to disown him. In this manner Melville represents the treatment he received from the world when he began cultivating the introspective tendencies of which he had recently become conscious. The death of Pierre's mother symbolizes the end of the influence on Melville's rational soul of the world that bred him. Discovery of Isabel's existence causes Pierre to reverse the ambiguously smiling portrait in his room to represent his "reversed idea" of his father; but he does not let it hang thus and stores it away.[53] Later he burns the portrait to ashes by casting it into the fire, an "eloquent symbol" of the "ultimate Truth itself."[54] Such was the fate suffered by Melville's early conception of God after he entered on his new course of reasoning. *Moby-Dick* gave evidence of the change. Pierre now exclaims: "Henceforth, cast-out Pierre hath no paternity, and no past; and since the Future is one blank to all; therefore, twice-disinherited Pierre stands untrammelledly his ever-present self!—free to do his own self-will and present fancy to whatever end!"[55] Pierre is here asserting what Melville had asserted about himself in a recent letter to Hawthorne, where he said that there was no power, natural or supernatural, which could infringe upon the sovereignty of his own being.[56] Ahab, one recalls, said the same of himself.[57]

Earlier there was much affection between Pierre and his prosperous cousin, Glen Stanly, who symbolizes Melville's public self. Glen had offered Pierre a house to live in if he should come to the city by the sea; but when Pierre appears in his changed condition, Glen will not acknowledge him. The infuriated Pierre and his women companions next have the horrible experience of being set upon by riff-raff from a brothel, an episode symbolizing an attack of fear and despair. Pierre soons finds quarters, however, in the Church of the Apostles. This property, once used for religious worship, now is inhabited chiefly by impractical idealists. Though humanity at large has little admiration for these men, Melville has a warm feeling for them. Pierre's lodging among them has an obvious significance.

In regard to the intimate relationship between Pierre and Isabel after they have moved to the city, it should be remembered that Isabel symbolizes the spiritual soul. Melville says: "Appalling is the soul of a man! Better might one be pushed off in the material spaces beyond the uttermost orbit of our sun, than once feel himself fairly afloat in himself!" He goes further to say: ". . . appallingly vacant as vast is the soul of man!"[58] The essence of this truth is expressed in Isabel's words to Pierre: ". . . all my life, all my full soul, contents not my brother."[59] Using a different figure, Melville observes: ". . . it is not for man to follow the trail of truth too far, since by so doing he entirely loses the directing compass of his mind; for arrived at the Pole, to whose barrenness only it points, there the needle indifferently respects all points of the horizon alike."[60]

In the beginning Pierre's good angel prompted him on the course that led to his self-renunciation for Isabel; his bad angel tempted him to ignore Isabel's message.[61] But in accord with the general ambiguity of the novel, the two angels exchange offices after Pierre has become involved; it is his good angel that would now save him from Isabel. When Lucy writes the letter saying that she is coming to join Pierre, she gives as the reason: ". . . a deep, deep voice assures me, that all noble as thou art, Pierre, some terrible jeopardy involves thee, which my continual presence only can drive away."[62] Upon learning of Lucy's coming, the jealous Isabel truthfully declares that Lucy is Pierre's good angel and that she herself is his bad angel.[63] After Lucy arrives, Pierre is "never alone with her; though, as before, alone with Isabel." Yet Lucy exerts a beneficent sway over him: "Pierre felt that some strange heavenly influence was near him, to keep him from some uttermost harm; Isabel was alive to some untraceable displacing agency."[64] Lucy's crayon-sketching promises to make her of aid in supporting the household; Isabel not only does nothing to help Pierre, but also begrudges him the time in which he works.[65]

Pierre's good angel, however, has come too late. The conflict between Melville's rational self and his reputation as an author is projected in the conflict between Pierre and Glen Stanly, who wishes to separate Lucy from Pierre's household. Here Melville represents the conflict within himself caused by knowing that the public wanted simple, objective books such as he felt he could no longer write. After being cut across the face by Glen's whip, Pierre shoots Glen. Thus Pierre's "own hand had extinguished his house in slaughtering the only unoutlawed human being by the name of Glendinning. . . ."[66] In publishing *Pierre* Melville knew that he was virtually destroying his contemporary fame.

At the end, in prison, Pierre reviews his life. The symbolism of the novel gives a tragic meaning to his words:

It is ambiguous still. Had I been heartless now, disowned, and spurningly portioned off the girl at Saddle Meadows, then had I been happy through a long life on earth, and perchance through a long eternity in heaven! Now, 'tis merely hell in both worlds. Well, be it hell. I will mould a trumpet of the flames, and, with my breath of flame, breathe back my defiance![67]

Pierre's breathing back his "breath of flame" is like Ahab's defiance of God: ". . . of thy fire thou madest me, and like a true child of fire, I breathe it back to thee."[68] If Melville had not become involved in introspection and had merely continued to develop his objective tendencies, he might have enjoyed the normal happiness of other men. As it was, his effort to arrive at the ultimate truth had brought him to such an unhappy state that now he defied the Deity. One wonders when Melville drew lines around the verse in his copy of the Psalms which reads: "Many there be which say of my soul, There is no help for him in God. Selah."[69] The next verse is not marked: "But thou, O lord, art a shield for me; my glory, and the lifter up of my head."

What happened in Melville's religious life is indicated

in the explanation given in regard to Pierre's vision of Enceladus, the Titan who attempted to storm heaven. In the dream Pierre sees his own face on Enceladus' trunk. Melville interprets:

Old Titan's self was the son of incestuous Coelus and Terra, the son of incestuous Heaven and Earth. And Titan married his mother Terra, another and accumulatively incestuous match. And thereof Enceladus was one issue. So Enceladus was both the son and grandson of an incest; and even thus, there had been born from the organic blended heavenliness and earthliness of Pierre, another mixed, uncertain, heaven-aspiring, but still not wholly earth-emancipated mood; which again, by its terrestrial taint held down to its terrestrial mother, generated there the present doubly incestuous Enceladus within him; so that the present mood of Pierre—that reckless sky-assaulting mood of his, was nevertheless on one side the grandson of the sky.[70]

Pierre's "heaven-aspiring, but still not wholly earth-emancipated mood" gives rise to his "sky-assaulting mood" by uniting with the earth-substance symbolized by Isabel; here again the bondage of the spiritual soul to the vegetal soul comes in. Isabel takes the place of Pierre's mother in the incestuous relationship. Though his art is rather weak here, Melville does give clues as to the symbolical relationship of Isabel and Mrs. Glendinning. In the early part of the novel Pierre habitually calls his mother "sister."[71] And since references both here and in other works show that Melville thought of the eyes as windows and the body as the house,[72] it is significant that the room in which Pierre confidentially talks with his mother and that in which Isabel tells him her story both are rooms with double casements.[73] One of the most effective scenes in the book is that representing Melville's first real communion with the spiritual soul: Isabel rhythmically in simple words tells of her weird, unhappy life as the soft heat-lightnings flash through the casement and the monotonous footsteps of Delly come from the room above like the beating of the pulse.[74] As in the myth Isabel takes the place of earth, Pierre's incest with her symbolizes the turning of the mind in upon itself. It was Melville's excessive introspection that gave rise to his "sky-assaulting mood."

The failure of Lucy's attempt to help Pierre support his household is in accord with the rest of the symbolism. When Lucy drew sketches in the country, before Pierre became involved with Isabel, two of the three legs of her easel were inserted in earth-filled pots, from which vines grew about the frame.[75] When Lucy comes to the city, Pierre curses on seeing that the vines have been torn from the easel: the generative power of the sensible soul is gone.[76] Lucy works on a portrait of Pierre, but at the end she has drawn no more than the skeleton.[77] Lucy's death in the last act of the drama symbolizes the death in Melville's being of the principle she represents. The fact that Melville wrote other books after *Pierre* is beside the point; he thought at the time of completing *Pierre* that his creative life was over.

On discovering that Lucy is dead, Pierre cries:

"Girl! wife or sister, saint or fiend!"—seizing Isabel in his grasp—"in thy breasts, life for infants lodgeth not, but death-milk for thee and me!—The drug!" and tearing her bosom loose, he seized the secret vial nestling there.[78]

That the drug they drink is nothing more than time is indicated symbolically in the last paragraph of the book, where the empty vial is compared to "a run-out sand-glass."

To use figures that Melville had used earlier, he felt that the avenging furies pursuing him at the end of *Mardi* were now almost on him; it would be only a brief time before the flower should fall to mold, before the ship should come to wreck. His excessive introspection had brought him to the point where he saw disaster immediately ahead.

And what was the cause of this: who was to blame?

He had built up a very dramatic case for himself in the three years between the publication of *Mardi* and the publication of *Pierre*. Pierre, the symbol of his own rational faculty, is represented as a noble, unselfish youth who sacrifices all to help an outcast girl whom he feels morally obligated to help. Melville says it is true Pierre was aware that, "in a transcendent degree, womanly beauty, and not womanly ugliness, invited him to champion the right."[79] But Pierre is consistently represented as acting *consciously* from the purest altruism: he renounces this prospect of earthly comfort and happiness for what he believes to be right. After he has set out on his course, he reads in Plinlimmon's pamphlet that whoever completely sacrifices himself for any person, thing, or idea is liable ultimately to run into peculiar forms of evil unthought of before. Pierre, however, is represented as not fully comprehending the central idea of the pamphlet at the time of reading it.[80] Much of the ambiguity of the novel hinges on this point. At the end Pierre calls himself "the fool of Truth, the fool of Virtue, the fool of Fate."[81] According to the presentation of Pierre, Melville sacrificed himself to reasoning on reality because in the beginning he considered it right to do so.

But one has to consider also the earlier symbolical record that Melville left of his spiritual life. In *Mardi* Melville represented Taji as having pangs of conscience over murdering the priest Aleema in rescuing Yillah. Had his deed "sprung of a virtuous motive," or had he selfishly wanted the beautiful maiden? Later he admits that he concealed himself from himself by covering his motives "with a gracious pretence." Finally he confesses that he committed the crime to gain the maiden and "would slay again to bring her back."[82] Taji is warned of the danger of following Yillah, but he willfully keeps on. According to this account of his pursuit of introspection, Melville does not show up to such advantage as in *Pierre;* for here one sees selfishness in his motivation. It is possible that in *Pierre* he was more concerned over writing a dramatic story than over adhering strictly to the facts of his spiritual history. It is also possible that by the time he wrote *Pierre* Melville had rationalized his actions to the point of really believing that he acted from the noblest impulses when he gave up certain normal worldly joys to devote himself to introspective reasoning. At any rate, with the earlier record as it is, one cannot help thinking that in Melville's cultivation of his subjective tendencies there was a certain amount of reckless self-indulgence.

Obviously Melville's writings were influenced by Byron, Shelley, and other romanticists;[83] and in the role of one who pursued the ultimate truth though he foresaw the harmful consequences, Melville himself looks somewhat like the Byronic hero. But religious influences were chiefly responsible for his original efforts to discover truth: ". . . ye shall know the truth, and the truth shall make you free." It was the desire to learn all that the human mind can know about God and the universe that led Melville first to explore the mind. It was the pursuit of truth that caused him to ignore the limits of human reason.

One of the shrewder contemporary judgments of Melville appeared in an article by Fitz-James O'Brien in 1857:

The sum and substance of our fault-finding with Herman Melville is this. He has indulged himself in a trick of metaphysical and morbid meditations until he has almost perverted his fine mind from its healthy productive tendencies. A singularly truthful person—as all his sympathies show him to be—he has succeeded in vitiating both his thought and his style into an appearance of the wildest affectation and untruth. His life, we should judge, has been excessively introverted. Much as he has seen of the world, and keen as his appreciation is of all that is true and suggestive in external life, he has turned away habitually, of late years, at least, to look in upon his own imaginations, and to cultivate his speculative faculties in a strange loose way.[84]

Just after Melville published *Pierre,* his family became very much worried about his health. He had worked himself into such a nervous state that his family, not understanding the symptoms, had him examined for insanity. The physicians pronounced him sane and assumed responsibility for his actions. Though his nervousness resulted in some unpleasantness for him and his relatives, no one familiar with valid tradition about Melville's state during this period has any doubts about his sanity.[85] In a recent article Sealts has shown how Melville symbolically told the story of his examination in "I and My Chimney," published in 1856. The chimney, which symbolizes Melville's mind, proves a sound piece of masonry with a broad foundation; instead of allowing it to be removed, the narrator says, "I and my chimney will never surrender."[86]

At the time he completed *Pierre,* Melville's disillusionment in God and man had brought him to the nadir of despondency. He was now farther from religious peace than he had ever been before.

CHAPTER VII

THE LONG SEARCH FOR PEACE

As WILLARD THORP observes in "Herman Melville's Silent Years," Melville was not so silent during his last forty years as some of his critics have intimated he was.[1] After the critical spring following the publication of *Pierre*, and after Melville's friends proved unable to get him a consular appointment, Melville began writing again. Among other activities during the first decade of the period after 1852, he wrote and published two novels and several stories and sketches, he saw other authors on various occasions, he went on two long voyages, and he delivered a number of lectures. After he published *Battle-Pieces* (1866), serving as a customs inspector for nineteen years kept him from devoting much time to writing; but he did publish *Clarel* (1876), and at the end of his life he wrote a good many pieces, among them the superb novelette *Billy Budd*.

Melville's life after 1852 was of course not so happy as it had been in the eighteen-forties, when, with bright prospects before him, he had written vigorously and had led an active social life. Several factors made his later life less happy. For one thing, his health was now not so robust as it had been. In addition to the rheumatism that afflicted him after 1855,[2] Mrs. Melville's letters show that on occasion nervousness and mental suffering recurred later, though not to so great a degree as just after *Pierre* was published.[3] Melville's failure as a self-supporting author also had its effect on his general outlook.

But among these and various other causes which contributed to his pessimism, his failure to find any satisfactory religious or philosophical explanation of the universe stands out as the most significant. This last portion of his life presents the pathetic enigma of one who, unable to reconcile himself to the loss of his early faith, spent much time reasoning on the same old problems. In the account of Melville's condition quoted at the beginning of this study, Hawthorne told how Melville, in 1856, said that he had about given up the thought that his soul was to retain its identity beyond this life; but Hawthorne saw that Melville could not "rest in that anticipation" and never would rest until he got "hold of a definite belief." Hawthorne was puzzled by Melville's persistence in taking up questions over and over, only to get the same unhappy answers. "He can neither believe, nor be comfortable in his unbelief; and he is too honest and courageous not to try to do one or the other. If he were a religious man, he would be one of the most truly religious and reverential; he has a very high and noble nature, and better worth immortality than most of us."[4] Melville's writing "Good talk" in his journal in regard to this conversation with Hawthorne shows that, as in earlier years, he enjoyed such discussion.[5] In the same journal, kept when he was in the Holy Land and Europe in 1856-1857, he noted, "Conversations with the Colonel on fixed fate &c. during the passage."[6] T. M. Coan told of visiting Melville with the hope of hearing him talk about his experiences in the South Seas and of hearing instead a philosophical monologue;[7] and Mrs. Metcalf says that sometimes in his later life Melville let the dinner grow cold while he held forth in Coleridgean manner. There is, of course, plenty of evidence that he could and did take part in ordinary conversation; the instances cited show merely that the characteristic which Hawthorne noted, of Melville's tendency to wander to and fro in "dismal and monotonous" metaphysical regions, occasionally manifested itself to others.

The gloominess of Melville's spiritual state during the latter part of his life is revealed perhaps most forcibly in the journal in which he recorded his thoughts on his visit to the Holy Land and in his long poem *Clarel*. Melville went to the Holy Land in an effort to recapture the true spirit of Christianity: the journal shows that all he found was disillusionment. "No country," he noted, "will more quickly dissipate romantic expectations than Palestine—particularly Jerusalem." He wondered if the "desolation" of Palestine were "the result of the fatal embrace of the Deity." The great quantity of stones in Judea made him understand more readily the numerous scriptural references to stones. He saw the "Cave of Jeremiah" and observed that in its "lamentable recesses" Jeremiah "composed his lamentable lamentations." He felt that as Haddon Hall suggested to Mrs. Radcliffe her "curdling romances," so "the landscape of Judea must have suggested to the Jewish prophets their ghastly theology."[8] The mercenary guides had little respect for the feelings of their Western patrons: in one breath they directed attention to "the arch where Christ was shown to the people" and to the place where "the best coffee in Jerusalem" was sold; "here is the stone Christ leaned against, & here is the English Hotel." The Church of the Holy Sepulchre disgusted Melville: it was "a show-box. All is glitter & nothing is gold. A sickening cheat. The countenances of the poorest & most ignorant pilgrims would seem tacitly to confess it as well as your own."[9] Such comments, together with incidental notes on his spiritual state, make his journal one of the most depressing records of travel ever written.

As for *Clarel*, into this poem of over five hundred pages Melville instilled virtually all the theological problems and arguments that had occupied his mind from the time he began to doubt. *Clarel* therefore seems rather strange when set among the religious poems of the time expressing the faith of Whittier, Holmes, Longfellow, and Lowell, though Lowell's "The Cathedral" offers several points of comparison. The various skeptics in the poem—Celio, Rolfe, Vine, Mortmain, Ungar, Clarel—serve merely as mouthpieces for Melville's own perplexities, somewhat as characters in *The Excursion* express Wordsworth's views. The fact that with all their philosophizing Melville's characters reach no joyful conclusions is therefore as one would expect.

Together with his novels, stories, shorter poems, and letters, and the marked and annotated volumes from his library, *Clarel* and the journal afford a great deal of material for the study of Melville's later thought. But since a detailed account of this material would involve repetition of much that has been said in previous chapters, and since, frankly, Melville's thought after 1852 seems to me much less interesting than his earlier thought, the purpose here is to note only the main trends during the later period.

One significant development is a more critical attitude toward science. Melville had written nothing so bitter on science or the scientific spirit in letters as a passage in the journal of 1856-1857 denouncing D. F. Strauss, whose *Life of Jesus* was a renowned piece of "higher criticism," and B. G. Niebuhr, whose incisive studies of Rome caused him to be called "the founder of historical criticism."[10] After seeing the isle of Patmos, Melville wrote:

Was here again affected with the great curse of modern travel—skepticism. Could no more realize that St. John had ever had revelations here, than when off Juan Fernandez could believe in Robinson Crusoe according to DeFoe. When my eyes rested on arid heighth, spirit partook of the barrenness.—Heartily wish Niebuhr & Strauss to the dogs.—The deuce take their penetration & acumen. They have robbed us of the bloom. If they have undeceived any one—no thanks to them.[11]

This passage is pathetic in that it shows momentary failing of the moral courage, but it testifies to Melville's intellectual honesty. In lamenting the destruction of old legends, Melville later said that these brought the sky nearer to some men—

> Did nearer woo it to their hope
> Of all that seers and saints avow—
> Than Galileo's telescope
> Can bid it unto prosing Science now.[12]

Between the time of his visit to the Holy Land and the publication of *Clarel*, in 1876, science made tremendous advances as an influence on the intellectual life of Europe and the United States. It was only two years after Melville's return from the Holy Land that Darwin's *Origin of Species*, to use Andrew D. White's phrase, came "into the theological world like a plough into an ant-hill."[13] In the strife that followed, in which theologians, like men of science, were divided in their attitude toward Darwinism, Melville was aware of the deification of science in some quarters. Henry Kalloch Rowe, in his *History of Religion in the United States*, writes: "Many scientists were so enamored of their facts and hypotheses that they claimed too much. They seemed to take pleasure in the destruction of that which was old. They inclined towards a materialistic explanation of all phenomena to the exclusion of spiritual reality altogether."[14] It is scientists of this type that Melville derides in *Clarel* in the character of Margoth, a Jewish geologist who says that "all's geology," and who would do away with the "old theologic myth." Because of Margoth's insensibility to spiritual things, the pilgrims condemn him severely, and Melville adds an extra touch by causing an ass to bray after certain of Margoth's speeches.[15]

Science, Melville said, enlarges the bounds of knowledge about the world, but leaves the human mind as helpless as always before religious mysteries. Science simply makes one more conscious of his ignorance about spiritual matters. It deals with nature, not God. In the Epilogue to *Clarel* Melville says that although Despair scrawls his "bitter pasquinade" on the brow of the calm Sphinx,

> Faith (who from the scrawl indignant turns)
> With blood warm oozing from her wounded trust,
> Inscribes even on her shards of broken urns
> The sign o' the cross—*the spirit above the dust!*

> Yea, ape and angel, strife and old debate—
> The harps of heaven and dreary gongs of hell;

> Science the feud can only aggravate—
> No umpire she betwixt the chimes and knell:
> The running battle of the star and clod
> Shall run for ever—if there be no God.
>
>   Degrees we know, unknown in days before;
>   The light is greater, hence the shadow more. . . .[16]

No amount of enlightenment about the physical world can keep the mass of men from being religious. As it is expressed by Rolfe, one of the most earnest and intelligent characters in the poem:

> Though some be hurled
> From anchor, nor a haven find;
> Not less religion's ancient port,
> Till the crack of doom, shall be resort
> In stress of weather for mankind.
> Yea, long as children feel affright
> In darkness, men shall fear a God;
> And long as daisies yield delight
> Shall see His footprints in the sod.
> Is't ignorance? This ignorant state
> Science doth but elucidate—
> Deepen, enlarge. But though 'twere made
> Demonstrable that God is not—
> What then? it would not change this lot:
> The ghost would haunt, nor could be laid.[17]

Such reasoning made Melville appreciate more than he had formerly the service of the Roman Catholic Church in harboring men from doubt and bewilderment. During his earlier career as an author he had shown a broadminded tolerance toward Catholicism, but he had also written jesting and seriously critical passages about it. The wave of thought caused by the Oxford movement, together with Melville's reaction to what he saw in Italy in 1857, probably had something to do with his more kindly attitude toward Catholicism in *Clarel*. In Italy he visited many cathedrals and chapels, and recorded "the stunning effect of a first visit to the Vatican."[18] Lowell said that when he went to see the cathedral at Chartres he hardly "saw the minster for the thoughts it stirred."[19] One of the passages Melville marked in Arnold's *Essays in Criticism* reveals that the "setting and outward circumstance" in Catholicism "have, it cannot be denied, a nobleness and amplitude which in Protestantism is often wanting to them."[20]

Men get "tired at last of being free," says Rolfe; they grow sick of the pain of endless philosophizing. And as a result of this in the past, not Protestantism and Liberalism have gained:

> Rome and the Atheist have gained:
> These two shall fight it out—these two;
> Protestantism being retained
> For base of operations sly
> By Atheism.[21]

The Dominican friar, with whom the pilgrims converse in passing, gives the most persuasive exposition of Catholicism. He says it is the fervors of the heart that

> Rome culls, adapts, perpetuates
> In ordered rites. 'Tis these supply
> Means to the mass to beautify
> The rude emotion; lend meet voice
> To organs which would fain rejoice
> But lack the song; and oft present
> To sorrow bound, an instrument
> Which liberates. Each hope, each fear
> Between the christening and the bier
> Still Rome provides for, and with grace
> And tact which hardly find a place
> In uninspired designs.

Rome, he admits, needed reform in Luther's day, but reform came within the Church, which, beneath its "rigidities of form," still adjusts itself to new times.[22] The Dominican's views are criticized by some of the other pilgrims, but on the whole the Dominican is sympathetically treated. In view of what is said about Catholicism here, it seems pertinent that in Arnold's essay on "Irish Catholicism and British Liberalism" Melville later marked a passage expressing the belief that Catholicism has

a great future before it; that it will endure while all the Protestant sects (in which I do not include the Church of England) dissolve and perish. I persist in thinking that the prevailing form for the Christianity of the future will be the form of Catholicism; but a Catholicism purged, opening itself to the light and air. . . .[23]

While Melville yearned for the peace that Catholicism and Protestantism gave to many, his critical nature not only prevented him from attaining it, but also caused him to continue denouncing evils in organized Christianity which he had pointed out before. "The Two Temples," a narrative sketch written early in this period, contained such graphic satire on Grace Church in New York City, in comparing the service there with a theatrical performance, that the editor of *Putnam's Monthly Magazine* rejected it for fear of offending the religious public, particularly the congregation of Grace Church and its pompous and obese usher named Brown.[24] Later attacks on religious intolerance, bigotry, fanaticism, mammonism, and the like, were as severe though not so localized.

One of the most important things to note during the period after 1852 is the cynical turn in Melville's attitude toward man. Melville had never been exceedingly optimistic about man. In the section on Serenia in *Mardi*, where he set forth his most idealistic views about society, man is said not to be perfectible, but merely to have within him a "germ" of goodness which should be cultivated.[25] In his most ardent pleading for reform, as in *Redburn* and *White-Jacket*, Melville remained fully aware of the difficulty of effecting real improvement in mankind. In his earlier comments about man there had been occasional very pessimistic notes. There is something more than humor, for instance, in Babbalanja's comparing human beings in their activities on earth to vermin on an animal,[26] and in his suggesting that men are "idiot, younger sons of gods."[27] In *Moby-Dick*, where it is said that if you take man in the abstract, "he seems a wonder, a grandeur, and a woe," it is also observed: ". . . take mankind in mass, and for the most part, they seem a mob of unnecessary duplicates, both contemporary and hereditary."[28] *Pierre* enlarges on man's inability to choose between the greatest good and evil; and *Israel Potter* gloomily says that "Man attains not to the nobility of a brick, unless taken in the aggregate."[29]

But it is *The Confidence-Man* (1857) which expresses Melville's most cynical views on man. Instead of running to throw robes over the blemishes of man, as he advocated in *Moby-Dick*,[30] he deliberately uncovers the meanness and stupidity of man. One wonders how much his views were influenced by his reading. In *Israel Potter* there is a comparison of the patriarch Jacob, Hobbes of Malmesbury, and Benjamin Franklin which comments on their subtle understanding of human nature and their prudence.[31] *The Confidence-Man* contains much to bolster Hobbes's argument that all human actions are motivated by selfish impulses. References in the novel to Thucydides and Tacitus[32] indicate that Melville was impressed by the records of man's wickedness that he found in their histories; and the mention of Lucian and Juvenal[33] suggests two more likely influences among the many that affected Melville's opinions on man. Here and there the novel reminds one of Swift, to whom Melville had recently alluded.[34] Religious disillusionment must of course be counted among the major influences.

In his portrayal of the confidence man Melville presents religion in a very cynical light. It is the religious front of the confidence man that enables him to fleece so many passengers aboard the ironically named steamboat the *Fidèle*. Assuming the role of a philanthropist, he pretends to collect funds for the "Seminole Widow and Orphan

Asylum" and for the "World's Charity," the latter of which would abolish all earthly misery and convert all the heathen to Christianity.[35]　He inspires "Christian confidence" in his fellow men by quoting from the thirteenth chapter of I Corinthians (well marked in Melville's New Testament) such passages as "Charity thinketh no evil," "Charity suffereth long, and is kind," and "Charity believeth all things."[36]

To use the words of a verse in the Psalms that Melville marked, the confidence man is one of "the workers of iniquity, which speak peace to their neighbors, but mischief is in their hearts."[37]　In presenting the Reverend Mr. Falsgrave in *Pierre*, and twice in *Israel Potter*, Melville referred to the wisdom of the serpent and the gentleness of the dove which Christ advised his Disciples to use;[38] the confidence man is a living embodiment of the injunction.　He is described in the novel itself by a passage adapted from Ecclesiasticus—an apocryphal book of wisdom that had made a strong impression on Melville:

Believe not his many words—an enemy speaketh sweetly with his lips. . . .　With much communication he will tempt thee; he will smile upon thee, and speak thee fair, and say What wantest thou?　If thou be for his profit he will use thee; he will make thee bear, and will not be sorry for it.　Observe and take good heed.　When thou hearest these things, awake in thy sleep.[39]

The remarkable success of this hypocrite indicates the folly of human beings.　The *Fidèle* is a miniature world containing "all kinds of that multiform pilgrim species, man,"[40] and there is much truth in the judgment of the wooden-legged cynic who heatedly exclaims to a group of the passengers: ". . . you flock of fools, under this captain of fools, in this ship of fools!"[41]　In the set of Chapman's Homer which George Duyckinck gave to Melville in 1858, one is not surprised to find checked and underlined: "blind Confidence, (The God of Fools)."[42]　The only people who escape the toils of the confidence man are the distrustful and coldly prudent, and the presentation of the practical philosopher Mark Winsome shows that Melville had no particular love for this type of person.[43]   In this connection Melville's copy of Crabb Robinson's *Diary* contains an interesting annotation.   Robinson says Blake once told him "that careless people are better than those who, &c., &c." Melville finished the sentence by annotating: "are coldly, selfishly, and malignantly prudent—which is a truism to the wise."[44]

Melville's gloomy views about man appear here and there in writings which followed this novel.   In the journal of 1856-1857 he recorded items pertaining to the lasting selfishness of man, "the self-possession & confidence of knavery—the irresolution & perplexity of honesty," man's derision of patience and honesty, the use of religion to induce men to wickedness, and the like.[45]   *Clarel* contains a great deal on the miserable state of man and, particularly in Ungar's speeches, some pessimistic views on democracy.[46] Melville's reading likewise furnishes evidence on the subject.   In a volume of Emerson's essays Melville marked the sentence: "Trust men, and they will be true to you; treat them greatly, and they will show themselves great, though they make an exception in your favor to all their rules of trade"; and he annotated: "God help the poor fellow who squares his life according to this."[47]   He underlined in a volume of Shelley the phrase "this hellish society of men."[48]   And in the seven volumes of Schopenhauer that he obtained at the very end of his life he marked passages on man's being the only mendacious creature, on the vulgarity of society, on the opposition of the ignorant mass to truth, and numerous other such topics.[49]

Yet it would not do to say that Melville remained to the end as bitter as he had been when he wrote *The Confidence-Man*.   In that novel he was without pity in portraying men as contemptible or ridiculous.   Later, his pessimism was often tempered by sympathy. In the "Supplement" to *Battle-Pieces* (1866) he wrote with much feeling for his countrymen in distress. Those who had sought to perpetuate slavery "were not the authors of it, but (less fortunate, not less righteous than we) were the fated inheritors. . . ." He proposed: "Let us be Christians toward our fellow-whites, as well as philanthropists towards the blacks, our fellow-men. In all things, and toward all, we are enjoined to do as we would be done by."[50] The passages on man in *Clarel* are characterized more by despair and pity than by derision. One might hate mankind, as a character there says, if hatred did not dissolve in pity of man's fate.[51]

It was pointed out earlier that Melville's sympathy for man was due partly to the belief that we are all suffering here together largely through no fault of our own but because in the nature of things decreed by God it is impossible for us not to suffer. Argument was advanced in *Mardi* that some men are so constituted it is easier for them to be good than for others not to be evil; the quality of a pot depends on the clay that the potter used in making it.[52]

This idea reappears in later years. It is expressed quite pointedly in a comment on a passage in Arnold's *Essays in Criticism*. Arnold wrote that in Maurice de Guérin, in Keats, and in David Gray "the temperament, the talent itself, is deeply influenced by their mysterious malady. . . ."[53] Melville annotated: "So is every one influenced—the robust, the weak,—all constitutions—by the very fibre of their flesh, & chalk of the bones. We are what we were made." Further evidence on the point may be found in his lamenting "the fatality" that made James Thomson pessimistic,[54] and in his marking a passage in *The World as Will and Idea* which notes "how incredibly great is the inborn difference between man and man, in a moral and in an intellectual regard."[55]

An excellent example of Melville's placing the blame for man's evil on God himself is in the characterization of

Claggart, in *Billy Budd*. In presenting Claggart, Melville refers to Plato's definition of "Natural Depravity: a depravity according to nature," pointing out that it evidently applies to individuals, not, like Calvin's dogma, to all mankind.

> With no power to annul the elemental evil in himself, though he could hide it readily enough; apprehending the good, but powerless to be it; what recourse is left to a nature like Claggart's, surcharged with energy as such natures almost invariably are, but to recoil upon itself, and, like the scorpion for which the Creator alone is responsible, act out to the end its allotted part.[56]

If one wishes a more scientifically phrased indictment of God for the evil in human nature, he can find it in a speech by Mortmain in *Clarel:*

> Nearer the core than man can go
> Or Science get—nearer the slime
> Of Nature's rudiments and lime
> In chyle before the bone. Thee, thee,
> In thee the filmy cell is spun—
> The mould thou art of what men be:
> Events are all in thee begun—
> By thee, through thee!—Undo, undo,
> Prithee, undo, and still renew
> The fall forever![57]

Scientific determinism, one of the forces that made Holmes more charitable toward criminals, seems to have had some influence on Melville.

Such reasoning on the problem of evil, which had inspired the attack on the Deity in *Moby-Dick,* inspired other passages during the latter part of Melville's life. The speech of Clarel at the end of Melville's long poem voices a familiar note:

> Conviction is not gone
> Though faith's gone: that which shall not be
> Still *ought* to be![58]

And *Timoleon,* the poem that Melville privately printed in the last year of his life, contains a striking instance of what in *Clarel* is referred to as "tantalised and apprehensive Man" asking, "Wherefore ripen us to pain?"[59] Plutarch's "Life of Timoleon," which Melville almost certainly read,[60] gives the same biographical facts about the Corinthian patriot as constitute the framework of Melville's poem, but Plutarch says nothing of Timoleon's inveighing against the gods during the twenty years he was out of public favor as a result of having his tyrannical brother assassinated.   The climax of Melville's poem represents Timoleon as thinking:

> To second causes why appeal?
> Vain parleying here with fellow clods.
> To you, Arch Principals, I rear
> My quarrel, for this quarrel is with the gods.
>   Shall just men long to quit your world?
> It is aspersion of your reign;
> Your marbles in the temple stand—
> Yourselves as stony and invoked in vain?
>   Ah, bear with one quite overborne,
> Olympians, if he chide ye now;
> Magnanimous be even though he rail
> And hard against ye set the bleaching brow.
>   If conscience doubt, she'll next recant.
> What basis then?   O, tell at last,
> Are earnest natures staggering here
> But fatherless shadows from no substance cast?
>   Yea, are ye, gods?   Then ye, 'tis ye
> Should show what touch of tie ye may,
> Since ye, too, if not wrung are wronged
> By grievous misconceptions of your sway.
>   But deign, some little sign be given—
> Low thunder in your tranquil skies;
> Me reassure, nor let me be
> Like a lone dog that for a master cries.[61]

The note of pity stands out in this plea for enlightenment. The few remaining lines, which tell of Timoleon's winning new fame as a general in Sicily, say nothing about his thanking the gods for the change in his fortunes. The giving of thanks to the Deity is notably rare in Melville's works.

In *Clarel* Melville refers to the ancient Gnostic belief that Jehovah is the

> Author of evil, yea, its god;
> And Christ divine His contrary:
> A god was held against a god,
> But Christ revered alone.

Although the Gnostics no longer exist, their heresy reappears in a different guise. The hostile attitude toward the Deity is now indirectly manifested:

> . . . none say Jehovah's evil,
> None gainsay that He bears the rod;
> Scarce that; but there's dismission civil
> And Jesus is the indulgent God.[62]

As for Melville himself, though his reasoning on man's lot caused him to question the benevolence of God, the impression that the teachings of Jesus had made on him gave him hope that some of his gloomier rational conclusions were wrong. This hope persisted, it should be remarked, in spite of critical thoughts that he entertained about the authenticity of scriptural records on Christ and also about the good resulting from the coming of Christ. In his journal of 1856-1857 he referred to Satan's taking Jesus to a mountain top for a vision of the world, and added: ". . . the *thing itself* was in vision."[63] And he recorded that when sailing over the waters from which Venus is fabled to have risen, he found it "as hard to realize such a thing as to realize on Mt. Olivet that from there Christ rose."[64] Among old and new charges leveled at Christ in *Clarel* are that he made mankind discontented in this world by telling of another world; his teaching does not agree with what one learns in this life; worship of Christ has led to much strife; his parables are not clear, leaving many in doubt as to what he meant; and he does not comfort those who need him.[65]

Yet Christ's doctrine of love and his promise of immorality were among the lasting influences in Melville's life. After all the unhappy reasoning in *Clarel* come lines expressing the belief that a resigned life of the heart is wisest, and that keeping the heart with diligence may bring one life immortal:

> Then keep thy heart, though yet but ill-resigned—
> Clarel, thy heart, the issues there but mind;
> That like the crocus budding through the snow—
> That like a swimmer rising from the deep—
> That like a burning secret which doth go
> Even from the bosom that would hoard and keep;
> Emerge thou mayst from the last whelming sea,
> And prove that death but routs life into victory.[66]

Billy Budd, completed a few months before Melville's death, reaffirms the wisdom of resigning the heart to the fate of man. In this tragic narrative Melville attained more calmness in treating the problem of evil than he had ever attained before. The passage on the "natural depravity" of Claggart refers to the Deity as responsible for evil, but there is no railing at the Deity. Here Melville is concerned not with the question of *why* evil exists, but of *how* man should accept its intricate and desolating effect.

Captain Vere and the members of the drumhead court realize the "essential innocence" of Billy Budd; they know that Billy's accidentally fatal blow was struck with no intention of mutiny or homicide, but only because, during a moment of stress, the impediment in his speech prevented a normal reply to Claggart's false accusation. If "the heart" and "the private conscience" had a part in their reaching a verdict, Billy should be acquitted, says Vere, as he will be "at the Last Assizes"; but as officers on a man-of-war their duty is not to attempt analyzing such "a mystery of iniquity," but to enforce military law, "however pitilessly that law may operate."[67]   Though Melville says that it is not known what took place at the interview during which Vere told Billy of the death sentence, he conjectures that there was confidence and understanding: "The austere devotee of military duty, letting himself melt back into what remains primeval in our formalized humanity, may in the end have caught Billy to his heart, even as Abraham may have caught young Isaac on the brink of resolutely offering him up in obedience to the exacting behest."[68]   Billy realizes that Vere is more to be pitied than himself.   At the execution Billy's final words, his only words, are, "God bless Captain Vere!" As his body ascends, the fleecy clouds in the east, struck by the sun's first rays, are "shot through with a soft glory as of the fleece of the Lamb of God seen in mystical vision."[69]

The understanding chaplain does not despair at having failed to convert Billy to his own ideas about death and his belief in Christ; he feels that innocence is finer than religion.   The common sailors are so impressed by the beauty of Billy's character that years later a chip of the spar from which he was hanged is to them "as a piece of the Cross."[70] Billy's name, though not uttered in remorse, is on the dying lips of Captain Vere.   It is significant that Vere dies fighting for the forms of his world, the forms that had made him send Billy to death: he is killed when his ship, the *Indomitable*, encounters and ultimately defeats the *Athéiste*.

Thus Melville counseled resignation to the inscrutable laws of the universe.   Deeply as man may be grieved by the rigid and sometimes merciless working of these laws, his duty is to accept them and to lay about him doing the best he can.   There is no attempt here to justify the ways of God to man.   There is no trace of Emerson's optimistic view that good is gradually displacing evil.   But there is the belief, as Matthiessen puts it, "that though good goes to defeat and death, its radiance can redeem life."[71]   In this narrative about a common sailor, whose execution reminds one in certain obvious ways of the Crucifixion, the effect on Melville of the miraculous beauty of Christ's goodness is as apparent as in anything else he ever wrote.

Along with the manuscript of *Billy Budd*, Melville left at his death the manuscript of a character sketch entitled "Daniel Orme," which, as a symbolical self-portrait, is important for understanding Melville's spiritual state at the end. During the early part of his career as an author Melville had represented himself as sailing the seas of the mind in an effort to discover real truth. He had experienced much turbulent life on these seas, at one time coming almost to wreck. In the character sketch he uses the "water symbolism" again. Daniel Orme (Daniel, or me?), a retired "captain of the top," had been unsociable and moody during the latter part of his life at sea; powder marks on his face, together with his moodiness, made a few of his shipmates foolishly suspect that in early life he had been a pirate. Thus Melville symbolically hints at the unwarranted suspicion in regard to his own sanity. (The character symbolizing Melville's father in "I and My Chimney" was also rumored to have been a pirate; the delirium in which Allan Melville died caused some foolish remarks about his mental health.)[72] It is true, says Melville, that Daniel Orme "had once served on a letter-of-marque"—a private vessel commissioned by its government to prey upon ships of the enemy. Now that Daniel had given up his strenuous life and lived quietly in a seaport, close by the waters, little of his gruffness remained.

He had found a certain peace, but not peace without sadness:

After being ashore for a period, a singularity in his habits was remarked. At times, but only when he might think himself quite alone, he would roll aside the bosom of his darned Guernsey frock and steadfastly contemplate something on his body. If by chance discovered in this, he would quickly conceal all and growl his resentment.

The object of his contemplation, Melville reveals, was "a crucifix in indigo and vermillion tattooed on the chest and on the side of the heart. Slanting across the crucifix and paling the pigment there ran a whitish scar, long and thin, such as might ensue from the slash of a cutlass imperfectly parried or dodged." It is intimated that the scar was received by Daniel during naval service, when he had fought to repel boarders. Into these few sentences Melville compressed the most moving part of his own religious history.

As time passed, "the superannuated giant" mellowed down "into a sort of animal decay," which, in such hardy natures as his, "mostly affects the memory by casting a haze over it; not seldom, it softens the heart as well, besides more or less, perhaps, drowsing the conscience, innocent or otherwise."

But let us come to the close of a sketch necessarily imperfect. One fine Easter Day, following a spell of rheumatic weather, Orme was discovered alone and dead on a height overlooking the seaward sweep of the great haven to whose shore, in his retirement from sea, he had moored. It was an evened terrace, destined for use in war, but in peace neglected and offering a sanctuary for anybody. Mounted on it was an obsolete battery of rusty guns. Against one of these he was found leaning, his legs stretched out before him; his clay pipe broken in twain, the vacant bowl and no spillings from it, attesting that his pipe had been smoked out to the last of its contents. He faced the outlet to the ocean. The eyes were open, still continuing in death the vital glance fixed on the hazy waters and the dim-seen sails coming and going or at anchor near by.

As to his last thoughts, "let us believe that the animal decay before mentioned still befriended him to the close, and that he fell asleep recalling through the haze of memory many a far-off scene of the wide world's beauty dreamily suggested by the hazy waters before him."[73]   The beloved and scarred crucifix over the heart, the rusted guns, the smoked-out pipe, and the eyes at death open toward the sea—these strokes give us a portrait which shows in a serene light the essential qualities of the man.

NOTES

IN THE NOTES that follow, all references to Melville's writings, except as otherwise indicated, are to the Standard Edition of *The Works of Herman Melville* (London: Constable and Company, 1922-1924). Because of their frequent mention, Raymond M. Weaver's *Herman Melville, Mariner and Mystic* (New York, 1921) and Willard Thorp's *Herman Melville: Representative Selections* . . . (New York, 1938) are cited under their respective author's surnames only. Similarly, the abbreviation G.-L.C. has been used for citations of material in the Gansevoort-Lansing Collection in the New York Public Library.

CHAPTER I

1. *Journal up the Straits*, ed. R. M. Weaver (New York, 1935), p. 5, under Nov. 12.

2. Randall Stewart (ed.), *The English Notebooks by Nathaniel Hawthorne Based upon the Original Manuscripts in the Pierpont Morgan Library* (New York and London, 1941), pp. 432-433.

3. See Weaver, p. 47.

4. See the "Paternal Line of the *Melvill* Family, of Boston (Massachusetts)," genealogical notes written by Allan Melville in 1820, in the G.-L.C. Justin Wright Clarke, "Major Thomas Melville: A Sketch of His Life," *Columbian Centinel*, Oct. 30, 1832, pp. 15-16, says that Thomas Melville gave up his plan of entering the ministry because of poor health.

5. See Mrs. Thomas Melville's letter of Oct. 19, 1830, to her son Allan (G.-L.C.).

6. See his letters to his wife, dated June 30, 1779, and Aug. 27, 1811 (G.-L.C.).

7. See her letters to General Gansevoort; her Last Will and Testament; Allan Melville's letters to Peter Gansevoort, her son, dated Oct. 22, 1825; and Jan. 16, 1826; her son Peter Gansevoort's letters to her, dated July 21, 1819, and Dec. 29, 1825; her son Leonard H. Gansevoort's letter to her, dated May 17, 1812; and her son Herman Gansevoort's letter to Peter Gansevoort, dated Aug. 6, 1823. The inventory of her "personal property and effects," dated June 17, 1831, lists many volumes of sermons, psalm-books, and miscellaneous religious items (G.-L.C.).

8. *Towards the Twentieth Century* (New York, 1937), p. 115.

9. Letter to Peter Gansevoort, dated March 10, 1828 (G.-L.C.).

10. Letter dated May 12, 1818 (G.-L.C.).

11. See his letters to Peter Gansevoort, dated Feb. 10, 1827, and Dec., 1831 (G.-L.C.).

12. The copy in the G.-L.C. contains his autograph and Augusta Melville's.

13. *Justina; or, The Will: A Domestic Story* (New York, 1823); two vols. bound in one. In the copy in the G.-L.C. is pasted a piece of paper containing the inscription: "Mother read this alout [*sic*] to me. Fanny P. Melville."

14. Dr. Henry A. Murray tells me that he has found evidence as to the regular church attendance of Allan Melville's family.

15. In a letter to her son Gansevoort, June 1, 1837 (G.-L.C.).

16. The records give the date of her joining as April 6, 1832.

17. In a letter dated Jan. 10, 1933, that Mrs. Metcalf wrote to me of an account given to her by Mrs. Frances Melville Thomas. In her diary, under Sunday, Oct. 8, 1871, Mrs. Catherine Gansevoort Lansing tells of attending church while visiting in Gansevoort, and says that in the afternoon the Dutch Reformed minister called on Mrs. Maria Melville and her daughter, and that they had "a spicy talk about the state of the Church at Gansevoort" (G.-L.C.).

18. Weaver, pp. 69-71.

19. *Pierre*, p. 6.

20. See *Pierre*, p. 6, and *Redburn*, pp. 264, 261, 271, 226.

21. See *Omoo*, pp. 198, 267, 352.

22. This journal is now in the Harvard College Library. Weaver, pp. 283-304, gives a good deal of it.

23. In a letter to the author, dated Dec. 21, 1932.

24. The lines are dated May 8, 1869, and after Mrs. Melville's initials are the words: "A sermon of Dr. Bellows suggested these lines to me." This copy appears to be a transcription of an earlier copy, which is also in her Bible.

25. She marked Matthew 10:22 and 24:13; Acts 14:22; Romans 9:36; I Corinthians 13:7; James 5:8, 10, 11, 13; and Revelation 7:17. She acquired her Bible in 1837.

26. In a letter to Catherine Gansevoort Lansing, dated Jan. 9, 1884 (G.-L.C.). See also Victor Hugo Paltsits (ed.), *Family Correspondence of Herman Melville, 1830-1904, in the Gansevoort-Lansing Collection* (New York, 1929), pp. 36-37.

27. See Mrs. Lansing's diary for June 22, 1866, and for July 15 and 17, 1870; and see Helen Melville's letter to her brother Allan, dated March 18, 1831 (G.-L.C.). Augusta Melville's well-worn copy of *The Evening Hymn* (London: T. Nelson and Sons, 1857) contains newspaper clippings and hymns and prayers and a number of inscriptions which show that she kept it with her when traveling.

28. In regard to Tom, see Mrs. Lansing's diary for Jan. 12, 1862; Oct. 10, 1869; April 24, 1870; and March 8, 1884 (G.-L.C.).

29. See the letter written by Helen Melville to Augusta Melville, Feb. 12, 1872, and Mrs. Lansing's diary for Feb. 11, 1872 (G.-L.C.).

30. See Frederic Hathaway Chase, *Lemuel Shaw: Chief Justice of the Supreme Court of Massachusetts, 1830-1860* (Boston, 1918), pp. 313-315.

31. *Essays in Criticism* (Boston, 1865), p. 354. Melville acquired this volume in 1869. It is now in the Harvard College Library.

32. "Biblical Allusion in Melville's Prose," *American Literature*, XII, 185 (May, 1940).

33. Letter to Hawthorne in Julian Hawthorne, *Nathaniel Hawthorne and His Wife: A Biography* (Boston, 1885), I, 405; and see *Moby-Dick*, II, 181.

34. It is now in the Harvard College Library (usually referred to hereinafter as H.C.L.).

35. See *Clarel*, I, 295; II, 114-115, 265; and the satire in *Moby-Dick*, II, 105-107; and see *ibid.*, I, xiv; II, 102.

36. Charles Mackay (ed.), *The Book of English Songs* (London, n.d.), p. 130 (H.C.L.).

37. *Shelley Memorials: From Authentic Sources, Edited by Lady Shelley; To Which Is Added An Essay on Christianity, by Percy Bysshe Shelley* (Boston, 1859), p. 290. Melville acquired the book in 1868 (H.C.L.).

38. *Journal up the Straits*, pp. 107-108, under Feb. 5.

39. See *The Confidence-Man*, p. 167; and *Mardi*, II, 54.

40. See *Redburn*, p. 215; *Moby-Dick*, II, 82; *Clarel*, I, 274, 275, 280, and *passim*.

41. I am indebted to J. H. Birss for calling my attention to Melville's having owned these two books.

42. Luther Stearns Mansfield, *Herman Melville: Author and New Yorker, 1844-51* (doctoral dissertation at the University of Chicago, 1936), p. 196, quotes this from Evert Duyckinck's "Jottings," Oct. 1, 1856.

43. *Moby-Dick*, I, 144.

44. See *Redburn*, p. 262; *White-Jacket*, pp. 194, 207.

45. Quoted in Mansfield, *op. cit.*, p. 195, from a letter of Evert Duyckinck's to his brother George, March 18, 1848.

46. See Melville's letter to Evert Duyckinck, April 5, 1849, in the Duyckinck Collection in the New York Public Library. Thorp, pp. 373-375, has reproduced the letter.

47. See *White-Jacket*, p. 63; and *Mardi*, II, 54; *Moby-Dick*, I, xiv; *Pierre*, p. 191; *Billy Budd and Other Prose Pieces* (hereinafter referred to as *Billy Budd*), pp. 29, 289; *Poems*, p. 421.

48. *Pierre*, p. 497; *Clarel*, I, 20, 173; II, 235; *Poems*, p. 376; and *Billy Budd*, p. 11.

49. See *Clarel*, I, 234; II, 114, 230; *Billy Budd*, p. 11. When Melville used Ethan Allen as a character in *Israel Potter*, pp. 191-193, in 1856, he may have known only *A Narrative of Col. Ethan Allen's Captivity, Written by Himself*, for he presented Allen as a Christian. But anyhow before he wrote *Clarel* (1876), he must have become acquainted with *Reason, the Only Oracle of Man*, for in *Clarel*, II, 230, Allen's name is coupled with Lord Herbert's.

50. *Pierre*, pp. 235-239.

51. See Leon Howard, "Melville and Spenser—A Note on Criticism," *Modern Language Notes*, XLVI, 291-292 (May, 1931); and *White-Jacket*, p. 444; *Moby-Dick*, I, xiv; *Piazza Tales*, p. 8; and *Billy Budd*, p. 141.

52. *Mardi*, I, 344; II, 241; *Redburn*, pp. 244, 324, 356; *White-Jacket*, p. 35, etc.; and see Melville's copy of Shelley's *Essays, Letters from Abroad, Translations and Fragments*, ed. Mrs. Shelley (new ed.; London, 1852), I, 33. The volume is dated in Melville's hand 1873.

53. See Melville's letter to Evert Duyckinck, Feb. 14, 1849, in the Duyckinck Collection, New York Public Library (in Thorp, p. 370); and "The Coming Storm," in *Poems*, p. 105. Some of the markings and annotations in Melville's set of Shakespeare are discussed in Charles Olson, *"Lear and Moby-Dick,"* *Twice a Year*, I, 165-189 (Fall-Winter, 1938), and F. O. Matthiessen, *American Renaissance* (New York, 1941), pp. 412 ff.

54. See *Typee*, p. 170; and Melville's journal of 1849-1850, in the Harvard College Library (or Thorp, p. xxviii).

55. See *Israel Potter*, p. 59; *The Confidence-Man*, pp. 32-34, 324.

56. Plato and his dialogues are referred to more than twenty times. See Melville's letter to Evert Duyckinck, April 5, 1849, in Thorp, pp. 373-375.

57. *Mardi*, II, 54; *The Confidence-Man*, p. 256. Merton M. Sealts has discovered evidence that Melville knew Proclus in translation and was rather scornful toward him.

58. See William Braswell, "Melville's Use of Seneca," *American Literature*, XII, 98-105 (March, 1940).

59. See *Mardi*, II, 54; *Pierre*, pp. 368, 405; *The Confidence-Man*, p. 257; *Clarel*, I, 147; II, 243; and Melville's copy of the New Testament and Psalms, Acts 17:28.

60. See *Mardi*, I, 14; *Redburn*, pp. 254, 85; *Moby-Dick*, I, xiii; II, 245; *Clarel*, I, 128; etc.

61. *Moby-Dick*, I, 333; *Pierre*, pp. 276, 294; *The Confidence-Man*, pp. 65, 181; and *Clarel*, II, 106.

62. *Mardi*, I, 15, 204; *Pierre*, pp. 290, 390, 421; *Clarel*, I, 260; and see text above, pp. 62-63.

63. *Israel Potter*, p. 59; *Omoo*, p. 14; *Moby-Dick*, I, xv; *Pierre*, p. 372.

64. *Billy Budd*, p. 252; *White-Jacket*, p. 207; *Moby-Dick*, II, 59.

65. See *Redburn*, p. 377; and Melville's copy of *The World as Will and Idea*, III, 394 (H.C.L.).

66. *The World as Will and Idea*, I, xi.

67. See Melville's journal of 1849-1850 (or the quotation in Weaver, p. 288).

68. K. H. Sundermann, *Herman Melvilles Gedankengut* (Berlin, 1937), p. 109.

69. See Melville's copy of *Literature and Dogma* (New York, 1881), p. xxi (H.C.L.).

70. See *Mardi*, I, 9, 72; *Pierre*, p. 372; *Piazza Tales*, p. 53.

71. See Melville's letter to Hawthorne, in Weaver, p. 321, and *Clarel*, II, 31.

72. See his copy of *Germany* (New York, 1859), II, 348 (H.C.L.).

73. *Pierre*, p. 405.

74. See Melville's journal of 1849-1850 (or Thorp, p. xxviii, n.); Melville also refers to *Faust* in *White-Jacket*, p. 233, and to Eckermann's *Conversations with Goethe* in *Moby-Dick*, I, xix; II, 119. See also *Mardi*, I, 204; *Pierre*, pp. 290, 421-422; and Melville's letter to Hawthorne, in Weaver, pp. 323-324.

75. See *White-Jacket*, pp. 63, 193, 207; *Moby-Dick*, I, 236-237; *Billy Budd*, p. 389; and the journal of 1849-1850 (quoted in Weaver, p. 285).

76. *White-Jacket*, p. 49; *Journal up the Straits*, pp. 138, 160; *Billy Budd*, p. 3; and William Braswell, "Melville as a Critic of Emerson," *American Literature*, IX, 321-322 (Nov., 1937).

77. See Viola Chittenden White, *Symbolism in Herman Melville's Writings* (an unpublished doctoral dissertation at the University of North Carolina, 1934), p. 354, and *passim*, for a study which emphasizes perhaps too much the Byronism reflected in Melville's works.

78. See *White-Jacket*, p. 340; *Journal up the Straits*, p. 129; *Clarel*, I, 215; II, 108.

79. For information about the volume of Emerson's *Poems* given to Melville, I am indebted to Mr. Carroll Wilson. On the marked and annotated volumes of the essays, see Braswell, "Melville as a Critic of Emerson."

80. See the present study, pp. 55-56.

81. *Literary World*, IV, 291-293 (March 31, 1849).

82. *Ibid.*, IV, 370 (April 28, 1849).

83. See Melville's letter to James Billson, Jan. 22, 1885, [London] *Nation and the Athenaeum*, XXIX, 712 (Aug. 13, 1921). Billson sent Melville Thomson's *The City of Dreadful Night and Other Poems* (London, 1880) and *Essays and Phantasies* (London, 1881).

84. See *Clarel*, I, 55; II, 3. The quoted words are from a passage on Leopardi that Melville checkmarked in his copy of Schopenhauer's *The World as Will and Idea*, III, 401.

85. See *Moby-Dick*, I, 164-165, 337, and *passim*.

86. See *Mardi*, II, 109.

87. See text above, pp. 110-112.

88. *Journal up the Straits*, pp. 107-108.

89. See Sir James George Frazer, *The Belief in Immortality and the Worship of the Dead*, Vol. II (London, 1922), Index.

90. See *Mardi*, I, 15; *Moby-Dick*, I, 3, 235, 331; II, 104; *Pierre*, p. 405; *Clarel*, II, 235; *Poems*, pp. 264, 270.

91. See *Mardi*, II, 54; *White-Jacket*, p. 194; *Moby-Dick*, *passim*; *Poems*, p. 272; *Clarel*, II, 21, 176, 280.

92. *Mardi*, I, 13, 345; II, 336; *Pierre*, p. 41; *Piazza Tales*, p. 109; *Clarel*, I, 127; *Billy Budd*, p. 6; etc.

93. See *Pierre*, p. 497; *Israel Potter*, p. 109; *The Confidence-Man*, p. 34; *Moby-Dick*, I, xiii.

94. See *White-Jacket*, pp. 360, 377; *Pierre*, pp. 132, 406; *The Confidence-Man*, p. 181.

95. See *Redburn*, p. 123; *White-Jacket*, p. 339; *Moby-Dick*, I, 292; *Pierre*, p. 361; *Clarel*, I, 86; II, 30.

CHAPTER II

1. Romans 14:22.
2. *Mardi*, I, 344.
3. *Ibid.*, II, 301.
4. *Ibid.*, II, 122-123.
5. *Ibid.*, II, 123.
6. Julian Hawthorne, *op. cit.*, I, 405.
7. *Mardi*, II, 276-277.
8. *Moby-Dick*, I, 132-133.
9. *Pierre*, p. 231.
10. Rev. ed. (at least the 12th ed.); n.d., p. 51.
11. Julian Hawthorne, *op. cit.*, I, 405-406.
12. *Mardi*, II, 380; and see II, 303, 336, 351, 366, 367.
13. *Ibid.*, II, 366.
14. *Ibid.*, II, 370.
15. *Monsieur Pascall's Thoughts* (London, 1688), p. 202.
16. I do not know what text Melville used, but this quotation is obviously from Saint Évremond's letter of 1671 to the Mareschal de Crequi, which contains an important statement of Saint Évremond's religious views. See *The Letters of Saint Évremond*, ed. John Hayward (London, 1930), p. 144.
17. Julian Hawthorne, *op. cit.*, I, 404.
18. *Pierre*, p. 447.
19. *Mosses*, pp. 16, 60.
20. Julian Hawthorne, *op. cit.*, I, 404.
21. *Mardi*, I, 329.
22. *Ibid.*, II, 54.
23. *Ibid.*, II, 125. Such a passage explains Melville's being interested enough to mark in his New Testament and Psalms the familiar verse: "The fool hath said in his heart, There is no God" (Psalms 14:1).
24. *Mardi*, II, 111.
25. *Ibid.*, I, 268, and see II, 352, 255, 300, 124.
26. Weaver, pp. 323-324, 327-329.
27. In *Pierre* he ridicules Spinoza and Goethe and in *Clarel* he condemns pantheism as "false though fair." See *Pierre*, pp. 290, 421-422; *Clarel*, I, 23, 260.
28. *Mardi*, I, 14; II, 359.
29. *Typee*, pp. 264, 165.
30. *Mardi*, II, 250, 260.
31. *Ibid.*, II, 208, 47.
32. See *Works* (Centenary ed.; Boston, 1903-1904), I, 124.
33. *Mardi*, II, 359.
34. *Ibid.*, II, 124-125.
35. *Ibid.*, II, 359.
36. *Ibid.*, II, 21, and see II, 249.

37. *Ibid.*, II, 376.

38. "Mr. Parkman's Tour," *Literary World*, IV, 291 (March 31, 1849).

39. *Moby-Dick*, I, 144.

40. Weaver, p. 328.

41. *Mardi*, II, 123, 323.

42. *Ibid.*, II, 299

43. *Ibid.*, II, 21, 131.

44. Matthew 23:9.

45. Matthew 10:20.

46. Psalms 8:3-5.

47. I Corinthians 7:40.

48. Acts 17:28.

49. John 10:34-36.

50. "Our souls are like those orphans whose unwedded mothers die in bearing them; the secret of our paternity lies in their grave, and we must there to learn it" (*Moby-Dick*, II, 264).

51. Weaver, p. 34.

52. See *Mardi*, I, 346; II, 115, 125, 74, 252.

53. *Ibid.*, II, 33; *Moby-Dick*, I, 97, 108.

54. "Melville's 'Agatha' Letter to Hawthorne," *New England Quarterly*, II, 298 (April, 1929).

55. *Mardi*, I, 276.

56. *Ibid.*, I, 14; "Mr. Parkman's Tour," *Literary World*, IV, 291 (March 31, 1849).

57. *Mardi*, II, 296, 215.

58. *Ibid.*, II, 300.

59. *Moby-Dick*, I, 59.

60. *Mardi*, II, 300-301.

61. In *Mardi*, II, 54, Melville referred to "divine Plato"; and in a letter to E. A. Duyckinck, April 5, 1849, he referred to the *Phaedo;* see Thorp, p. 375. See the *Phaedo* and A. Seth Pringle-Pattison, *The Idea of Immortality* (Oxford, 1922), pp. 58-61.

62. *Mardi*, II, 374-377; and see I, 268.

63. *Ibid.*, I, 276, 272.

64. *Works*, XI, 436; and see Arthur Christy, *The Orient in American Transcendentalism* (New York, 1932), p. 111.

65. *Mardi*, I, 335-336.

66. *Ibid.*, I, 277.

67. *Ibid.*, I, 244.

68. Quoted by A. Seth Pringle-Pattison, *The Idea of God in the Light of Recent Philosophy* (2d ed.; New York, 1920), p. 44.

69. *Mardi*, II, 359, and see II, 302.

70. *The Confidence-Man*, p. 85.

71. See above, p. 15.

72. *Ibid.*, II, 79, and see Braswell, "Melville's Use of Seneca," pp. 102-103.

73. *Ibid.*, II, 303.

74. Weaver, p. 329.

75. *Billy Budd*, pp. 129-130.
76. *Typee*, p. 262; *Moby-Dick*, I, 5; and see *Mardi*, II, 385-386.
77. *Mardi*, II, 156.
78. *Ibid.*, II, 251.
79. *Typee*, pp. 269-270.
80. *Mardi*, II, 303.
81. Rousseau is mentioned in *Typee*, p. 170.
82. Thorp, p. cii.
83. For some of the more important passages in the early works on free will, fate, chance, necessity, and predestination, see *Mardi*, II, 121, 127; *White-Jacket*, pp. 311, 404-502; and *Moby-Dick*, I, 6-7, 252-253, 270; II, 48-49.
84. *Typee*, p. 273.
85. *Mardi*, II, 78, and see Melville's copy of Sir Roger L'Estrange's *Seneca's Morals by Way of Abstract* . . . (15th ed.; London, 1746), pp. 87-88 (G.-L.C.).
86. *Mardi*, II, 79-80.
87. See especially Charles Roberts Anderson, *Melville in the South Seas* (New York, 1939), chap. v; and see his bibliography and Thorp's for references to work by other scholars on Melville and the missionaries.
88. *Omoo*, p. 220.
89. *Typee*, p. 264.
90. *Omoo*, pp. 216-217.
91. *Ibid.*, pp. 211-213.
92. *Ibid.*, pp. 199-205.
93. *Ibid.*, pp. 142-147, 204, 167-170. In regard to Catholic sectarianism he says that instead of coming to Tahiti to work among people already nominally Christianized, the priests might better have gone to work among the unconverted (p. 147).
94. *Mardi*, II, 249. The rest of the material on Maramma is drawn from *ibid.*, II, 1-49 (chaps. i-xiii).
95. *Ibid.*, II, 31-32.
96. *Mardi*, II, 362. The rest of the material on Serenia is taken from chap. lxxxiii (II, 364-372).
97. *Typee*, p. 273.
98. Acts 2:44-45.
99. James 2:14, 18. And see John 12:47; John 8:24; John 5:24, 29; John 3:18, 36; John 10:8; Romans 4:5-6; Romans 10:9; some of these Melville could have marked only through disfavor, as they express ideas contrary to his own.
100. New York, 1881, p. 116.

CHAPTER III

1. See Weaver, p. 273.
2. In her journal Mrs. Melville noted: "Summer of 1849 we remained in New York. He wrote *Redburn* and *White-Jacket*"; Weaver, p. 304.

3. See Melville's journal for Nov. 6, 1849, quoted in Weaver, p. 292; and see his letter of Dec. 14, 1849, to E. A. Duyckinck, quoted in Thorp, pp. 376-377.

4. *Redburn*, pp. 176-177.

5. *Ibid.*, p. 379.

6. *Ibid.*, p. 237.

7. *Ibid.*, p. 227.

8. See *White-Jacket*, pp. 218, 112, on drunkenness; p. 383, on gambling; pp. 473-474, on sodomy; and pp. 166-189, 348-354, 465-469, on flogging.

9. Hugh W. Hetherington, *The Reputation of Herman Melville in America* (an unpublished doctoral dissertation at the University of Michigan [1933]), p. 168. See also Charles Roberts Anderson, "A Reply to Herman Melville's *White-Jacket* by Rear-Admiral Thomas O. Selfridge, Sr.," *American Literature*, VII, 142 (May, 1935).

10. *White-Jacket*, pp. 473-475.

11. See Albert Mordell, "Melville and 'White Jacket,' " *Saturday Review of Literature*, VII, 946 (July 4, 1931) and *White-Jacket*, p. 195. The *Church Almanac*, published annually in New York by the Protestant Episcopal Tract Society, briefly recorded Bartow's service as a chaplain. None of the biographical dictionaries, such as Appleton's, Lamb's, and the *D. A. B.*, contains an article on Bartow; and judging from such catalogues as Roorbach, he evidently published nothing.

12. *White-Jacket*, pp. 193-194.

13. *Ibid.*, p. 196.

14. *Billy Budd*, p. 100.

15. See *Deck and Port; or, Incidents of a Cruise in the United States Frigate Congress to California* (New York, 1850), pp. 19, 304, 317-318, on grog; pp. 58, 210, 223, and *passim*, on sermons; p. 23, on flogging; pp. 136, 384, on war.

16. See *ibid.*, pp. 183, 319, 390.

17. *White-Jacket*, p. 195.

18. *Ibid.*, pp. 363-364.

19. *Ibid.*, pp. 336, 434.

20. *Ibid.*, pp. 234, 262, 287, 403.

21. *Ibid.*, p. 177.

22. *Ibid.*, pp. 352-353.

23. *Ibid.*, p. 189, and see *Redburn*, pp. 216-217.

24. *White-Jacket*, p. 368.

25. *Ibid.*, p. 396.

26. *Ibid.*, p. 403, and see p. 262.

27. *Ibid.*, p. 408. See also text above, p. 81.

28. *Ibid.*, p. 504.

29. *Ibid.*, p. 404, and see p. 197.

30. Matthew 5:39.

31. *White-Jacket*, p. 403.

32. *Ibid.*, pp. 502-504.

33. See *ibid.*, p. 231.

34. *Ibid.*, p. 502.

35. *Mardi*, I, 14.

36. *Redburn*, p. 179.

37. See *Mardi*, II, 376.

38. *White-Jacket*, p. 311; and see *Redburn*, p. 134, on Jackson, who was "spontaneously an atheist and an infidel," and whose "wickedness seemed to spring from his woe."

39. *White-Jacket*, p. 234.

40. *Ibid.*, p. 394.

41. See *ibid.*, pp. 161, 231, 454-455, and *passim.*

42. *Southern Literary Messenger*, XVI, 250-252 (April, 1850).

43. *Literary World*, VI, 297-299 (March 23, 1850).

44. Hetherington, *op. cit.*, p. 168.

45. *Redburn*, p. 377.

46. The words are Joseph de Maistre's; quoted by J. B. Bury, *The Idea of Progress* (London, 1921), p. 118.

47. This letter is in the Duyckinck Collection, in the New York Public Library; the quoted passage is omitted from the reproduction of the letter in Minnigerode, *op. cit.*, pp. 8-9, but is included in Thorp, p. 375.

48. *Mardi*, II, 54; *Moby-Dick*, II, 116.

49. *The Dictionary Historical and Critical of Mr. Peter Bayle* (London, 1737), IV, 653.

50. *White-Jacket*, p. 194.

51. See *Redburn*, p. 261, and *Mardi*, II, 368.

52. Weaver, p. 294.

53. *Ibid.*, p. 300. According to the *D. N. B.*, Henry Melville (1798-1871) "for many years had the reputation of being 'the most popular preacher in London,' and one of the greatest rhetoricians of his time."

54. Weaver, p. 285. Melville's actual spelling of the italicized term, as it appears in the manuscript journal, is *"Colredegian."*

55. On this subject and especially on the friendship between Melville and Evert A. Duyckinck, see Mansfield, *Herman Melville: Author and New Yorker, passim.*

56. See *ibid.*, p. 196, n. 22.

57. See the article on George Duyckinck in *The Cyclopaedia of American Literature* (Philadelphia, 1875), II, 837, and Thorp, p. xxiii.

58. Mansfield, *op. cit.*, p. 35.

59. *Literary World*, VI, 297-299 (March 23, 1850).

60. Henry A. Beers, *Nathaniel Parker Willis* (American Men of Letters; Boston, 1913), pp. 94-95.

61. *Billy Budd*, pp. 127-131.

62. See Weaver, p. 328, and Julian Hawthorne, *op. cit.*, I, 398.

63. *The American Notebooks by Nathaniel Hawthorne*, ed. Randall Stewart (New Haven, 1932), p. 220.

64. See *ibid.*, pp. 133-134, 210, 147.

65. *Ibid.*, p. 165.

66. See her letter to E. A. Duyckinck, Aug. 29, 1850, in the Duyckinck Collection, in the New York Public Library.

67. Julian Hawthorne, *op. cit.*, I, 388.

CHAPTER IV

1. *Billy Budd*, p. 131.

2. *Ibid.*, I, 229-230.

3. *Ibid.*, II, 330.

4. *Ibid.*, II, 38.

5. *Ibid.*, I, 204.

6. See E.-D. Forgues, "Moby Dick, la Chasse à la Baleine, Scènes de Mer," *Revue des Deux Mondes*, I, 493 (23d year, Feb., 1853). Forgues, however, does not enlarge on the allegory.

7. *Moby-Dick*, II, 43.

8. *Ibid.*, I, 332; II, 104.

9. *Ibid.*, II, 83.

10. *Ibid.*, II, 334-335.

11. *Ibid.*, I, 224.

12. *Ibid.*, I, 226-227.

13. *Ibid.*, I, 229.

14. *Ibid.*, I, 243.

15. *Ibid.*, II, 365-366.

16. *Ibid.*, II, 275, 320, 55-56.

17. *Ibid.*, I, 273.

18. *Ibid.*, I, 211.

19. *Ibid.*, I, 233.

20. I Kings 16:33.

21. *Moby-Dick*, I, 210. See in *D. N. B.* the article on William Thompson (1811-1880), a pugilist known in the sporting press as "Bendigo."

22. *Ibid.*, II, 285.

23. Chap. cxix.

24. See F. Legge, *Forerunners and Rivals of Christianity* (Cambridge, 1915), II, 210-212.

25. *White-Jacket*, p. 194; Tertullian's tract is mentioned on this page. On Melville's knowledge of Bayle see above, pp. 51-52.

26. Julian Hawthorne, *op. cit.*, I, 388.

27. *Moby-Dick*, II, 282-283.

28. Matthew Arnold, *Essays in Criticism*, p. 251. The italics are in the text.

29. London, 1881, p. 308. Melville also marked in this volume (p. 303) a quotation from Hegel: "Would you be philosophers? commence by being Spinozists, else you can accomplish nothing."

30. See *Mardi*, I, 15, 204, and see also *Pierre*, pp. 290, 390, 421, and *Clarel*, I, 260.

31. Julian Hawthorne, *op. cit.*, I, 388.

32. *Moby-Dick*, I, 204.

33. *Ibid.*, II, 244.

34. *Pierre*, p. 306.

35. *Moby-Dick*, II, 71.

36. See George Santayana, *Reason in Religion* (New York, 1905), p. 156.

37. *Moby-Dick*, I, 152-153.

38. *Ibid.*, II, 281-282.

39. Julian Hawthorne, *op. cit.*, I, 404.

40. *Moby-Dick*, II, 301-302.

41. *Ibid.*, II, 352, and see II, 330, also.

42. See Achilles Madison Holt, "The Theme of *Moby-Dick* as Developed by Similes" (unpublished Master's thesis at Stanford University, 1937), p. 70; Yvor Winters, "Herman Melville and the Problems of Moral Navigation," in *Maule's Curse* (Norfolk, Conn., 1938), p. 63; and Thorp, p. lxxiii.

43. *Moby-Dick*, I, 252-253.

44. *Ibid.*, I, 91-92.

45. *Ibid.*, I, 115-116.

46. *Ibid.*, II, 352.

47. *Ibid.*, I, 209.

48. *Ibid.*, II, 258.

49. *Ibid.*, II, 339.

50. *Ibid.*, I, 154.

51. *Ibid.*, I, 209, and Stanley Geist, *Herman Melville: The Tragic Vision and the Heroic Ideal* (Harvard Honors Theses in English, No. 12; Cambridge, 1939), p. 47.

52. *Ibid.*, II, 328.

53. *Moby-Dick*, I, 149-150. See W. S. Gleim, *The Meaning of Moby-Dick* (New York, 1938), p. 122, on this point.

54. See *Moby-Dick*, I, 159; II, 265, 341.

55. *Ibid.*, II, 256, 181, 34; I, 236.

56. *Ibid.*, II, 310.

57. *Ibid.*, II, 181.

58. *Mardi*, II, 359, 376.

59. *Moby-Dick*, II, 281.

60. Julian Hawthorne, *op. cit.*, I, 388.

61. *Moby-Dick*, II, 366.

62. *Ibid.*, II, 119.

63. Percy Bysshe Shelley, *Essays, Letters from Abroad, Translations and Fragments*, I, 33.

64. On Melville's familiarity with *Paradise Lost*, see "Mr. Parkman's Tour," *Literary World*, IV, 292 (March 31, 1849); *Redburn*, pp. 244, 356; *White-Jacket*, p. 35; and *Moby-Dick*, I, xv.

65. *Moby-Dick*, I, 144.

66. *Ibid.*, I, 220.

67. *Ibid.*, II, 26.

68. William S. Ament, "Bowdler and the Whale," *American Literature*, IV, 39-46 (March, 1932), cites this as one of the many passages that the English editor's religious standards caused him to expurgate.

69. *Mardi*, I, 47.

70. *Ibid.*, I, 59.

71. *Ibid.*, I, 84.

72. *Ibid.*, I, 286.

73. Melville underlined these words in a quotation from Heine in his copy of Matthew Arnold, *Essays in Criticism*, p. 195.

74. Luther Stearns Mansfield, "Glimpses of Herman Melville's Life in Pittsfield, 1850-1851," *American Literature*, IX, 48 (March, 1937).

75. *Pierre*, p. 125.

76. *Ibid.*, p. 196.

77. Julian Hawthorne, *op. cit.*, I, 404.

78. *Pierre*, p. 441.

79. Both authors are referred to in *Pierre*, p. 497.

80. *The Confidence-Man*, pp. 184, 335-336.

81. Julian Hawthorne, *op. cit.*, I, 400.

82. *Moby-Dick*, II, 261. I have supplied the italics.

83. Weaver, p. 327.

84. See his letter to Hawthorne, in Julian Hawthorne, *op. cit.*, I, 388.

CHAPTER V

1. See *Shorter Novels of Herman Melville*, with an Introduction by Raymond Weaver (Black and Gold Library; New York, 1928), p. xxxiii.

2. See his letter to Evert Duyckinck, in Thorp, pp. 382-383; and see also the autobiographical passage on Pierre as author in *Pierre*, p. 473.

3. He represents Pierre as thinking that "could he now hurl his deep book out of the window, and fall to on some shallow nothing of a novel, composable in a month at the longest, then could he reasonably hope for both appreciation and cash. But the devouring profundities" would not then permit Pierre to be "entertainingly and profitably shallow in some pellucid and merry romance" (*Pierre*, p. 425).

4. See Melville's journal, in Weaver, p. 292, and his letter to Evert Duyckinck, in Thorp, p. 376.

5. See Julian Hawthorne, *op. cit.*, I, 402.

6. For more argument to support this theory, see my article "The Satirical Temper of Melville's *Pierre*," *American Literature*, VII, 424-438 (Jan., 1936).

7. See Leonard Burwell Hurley, *The American Novel, 1830-1850: Its Reflection of Contemporary Religious Conditions, with a Bibliography of Fiction* (unpublished doctoral dissertation at the University of North Carolina, 1932), I, 203; Herbert Ross Brown, *The Sentimental Novel in America, 1789-1860* (Durham, N. C., 1940), Bk. II, chap. v; and E. Douglas Branch, *The Sentimental Years, 1836-1860* (New York, 1934), chaps. iv and v.

8. See Brown, *op. cit.*, Bk. II, chap. v.

9. *Literary World*, IV, 370 (April 28, 1849).

10. *Pierre*, p. 343.

11. *Ibid.*, pp. 198-200.

12. *Ibid.*, pp. 43-46, 83.
13. *Ibid.*, p. 30.
14. *Ibid.*, pp. 89-90.
15. *Ibid.*, p. 125.
16. See *Redburn*, p. 227.
17. *Moby-Dick*, II, 230.
18. *Pierre*, pp. 135-145.
19. *Ibid.*, p. 230.
20. *Ibid.*, p. 148.
21. *Ibid.*, pp. 240-241.
22. *Ibid.*, p. 253.
23. *Ibid.*, pp. 150-151.
24. The pamphlet, with prefatory remarks, is contained in Book XIV of the novel, pp. 284-300.
25. *White-Jacket*, p. 408. In *Moby-Dick*, II, 170, Melville said in regard to the mad Negro boy Pip that "man's insanity is heaven's sense; and wandering from all mortal reason, man comes at last to that celestial thought, which, to reason, is absurd and frantic; and weal or woe, feels then uncompromised, indifferent as his God." See also text above, p. 47.
26. I Corinthians 3:18.
27. *Typee*, p. 266.
28. *Pierre*, p. 381.
29. See Julian Hawthorne, *op. cit.*, I, 40, and Shaftesbury, *An Inquiry concerning Virtue or Merit*, in *Characteristicks* (Birmingham, 1773), II, 90.
30. See Joseph Butler, *Sermons* (New York, 1844), pp. viii-ix, 35-36.
31. See *Pierre*, p. 289.
32. *Literary World*, XI, 119 (Aug. 21, 1852).
33. "Our Young Authors—Melville," *Putnam's Monthly Magazine*, I, 156 (Feb., 1853). (I have italicized the title of the novel in the quotation.) For an analysis of the contemporary reviews of *Pierre*, see Hetherington, *op. cit.*, pp. 294-300.

CHAPTER VI

1. Julian Hawthorne, *op. cit.*, I, 405-406.
2. *Redburn*, p. 322.
3. *The Anatomy of Melancholy*, Part I, sec. 1, mem. 2, subsecs. 1-11. The edition quoted here was published by Wiley & Putnam in 1847.
4. *Moby-Dick*, I, 133.
5. See *Mardi*, I, 13-19, 170-171.
6. *The Works of Plato*, trans. Floyer Sydeham and Thomas Taylor (London, 1804), IV, 266.
7. *Mardi*, II, 54.
8. *Ibid.*, I, 159, 171.
9. *The Works of Plato*, I, 244-245.
10. *Mardi*, I, 182.
11. *Ibid.*, I, 168, 186.
12. *Ibid.*, I, 220.

13. *Ibid.*, I, 160.

14. *Ibid.*, I, 226.

15. *Ibid.*, I, 162.

16. *Ibid.*, I, 184-185.

17. See *Redburn*, p. 377; Melville referred to Hobbes as early as in *Omoo*, p. 14, and Locke as early as in *White-Jacket*, p. 207.

18. *Mardi*, I, 357-358.

19. *Ibid.*, I, 182.

20. Homans, *op. cit.*, p. 709.

21. *Mardi*, I, 185.

22. *Ibid.*, II, 395.

23. *Ibid.*, II, 393.

24. *Ibid.*, I, 157.

25. *Ibid.*, I, 162.

26. *Ibid.*, II, 118.

27. *Ibid.*, II, 380.

28. *Ibid.*, II, 277.

29. *Ibid.*, II, 400.

30. See Dr. Henry A. Murray's review of Mumford's *Herman Melville*, in the *New England Quarterly*, II, 523-526 (July, 1929).

31. *Pierre*, p. 93.

32. In writing of these two portraits, Melville, as is now well known, described two very different portraits of his own father.

33. *Pierre*, p. 99.

34. *Ibid.*, p. 115.

35. *Ibid.*, p. 58.

36. *Ibid.*, p. 70.

37. *Ibid.*, p. 243.

38. *Ibid.*, p. 266.

39. *Ibid.*, p. 451.

40. *Ibid.*, pp. 212-213.

41. *Ibid.*, p. 160.

42. *Ibid.*, p. 167.

43. *Ibid.*, p. 393.

44. *Ibid.*, p. 177.

45. *Ibid.*, p. 178.

46. *Ibid.*, pp. 381-382, and see p. 215.

47. *Moby-Dick*, I, 133.

48. *Pierre*, p. 215.

49. *Mardi*, II, 123.

50. *Pierre*, p. 164.

51. *Ibid.*, pp. 33-34.

52. *Ibid.*, p. 15. Melville's italics.

53. *Ibid.*, p. 121.

54. *Ibid.*, pp. 276, 306.

55. *Ibid.*, p. 277.

56. Julian Hawthorne, *op. cit.*, I, 388.

57. *Moby-Dick*, II, 281.
58. *Pierre*, pp. 396-397.
59. *Ibid.*, p. 435.
60. *Ibid.*, p. 231.
61. *Ibid.*, p. 87.
62. *Ibid.*, p. 433.
63. *Ibid.*, pp. 437-438.
64. *Ibid.*, pp. 469-470.
65. *Ibid.*, pp. 459, 463-465, 485.
66. *Ibid.*, p. 502.
67. *Ibid.*, p. 502.
68. *Moby-Dick*, II, 282.
69. Psalms 3:2.
70. *Pierre*, p. 483.
71. *Ibid.*, pp. 4, 17, 18, 22, and *passim*.
72. See *Moby-Dick*, I, 11; II, 61; *Typee*, p. 293; *Pierre*, p. 475.
73. *Pierre*, pp. 265, 257, 269.
74. *Ibid.*, pp. 160, 166, 168, 172, 175, 201, 218.
75. *Ibid.*, p. 52.
76. *Ibid.*, p. 443.
77. *Ibid.*, p. 499.
78. *Ibid.*, p. 503.
79. *Ibid.*, p. 151.
80. See *ibid.*, p. 291.
81. *Ibid.*, p. 499.
82. *Mardi*, I, 157, 162; II, 118.
83. On this point see above, p. 16, and Viola Chittenden White, *Symbolism in Herman Melville's Writings*, pp. 281, 354, 370, and *passim*.
84. Fitz-James O'Brien, "Our Authors and Authorship. Melville and Curtis," *Putnam's Monthly Magazine*, IX, 390 (April, 1857).
85. I base this statement on personal talks with Mrs. Eleanor Melville Metcalf and with Professor Raymond Weaver. Melville's wife late in life jotted in her diary: "We all felt anxious about the strain on his [Melville's] health in the spring of 1853" (quoted in Weaver's Introduction to Melville's *Journal up the Straits*, p. xv).
86. See Merton M. Sealts, "Herman Melville's 'I and My Chimney,'" *American Literature*, XIII, 142-154 (May, 1941).

CHAPTER VII

1. Willard Thorp, "Herman Melville's Silent Years," *University Review*, III, 254-262 (Summer, 1937), gives a good account of Melville's later life.
2. See Weaver, p. 352.
3. See her letters, of 1876 and 1877, in Paltsits, *op. cit.*, pp. 35-36, 38, 46, 50.
4. Julian Hawthorne, *op. cit.*, II, 135.
5. *Journal up the Straits*, p. 5, under Nov. 12.
6. *Ibid.*, p. 1.

Notes

7. See his letter in Weaver, p. 351.

8. Preceding "ghastly," Melville wrote and lined out, "terrific, diabolical, terrible." The terrible aspect of the Egyptian pyramids made him conclude with a shudder that in the pyramids "was conceived the idea of Jehovah" (see the journal under Jan. 3, "Pyramids").

9. See under "Jerusalem" in the journal.

10. Antoine Guillard, *Modern Germany and Her Historians* (New York, 1915), p. 40.

11. See journal under Feb. 5.

12. *Clarel*, I, 142. Lowell, in "The Cathedral," ll. 376-379, comments on the "nineteenth century with its knife and glass" which "make thought physical" and thrust heaven afar.

13. *A History of the Warfare of Science with Theology in Christendom* (New York, 1910), I, 70.

14. *History of Religion in the United States* (New York, 1924), p. 134.

15. *Clarel*, I, 278, 249, 311-312. Vine, who sits apart from the others, may possibly be doing the "braying."

16. *Clarel*, II, 297, and see II, 24.

17. *Ibid.*, I, 126.

18. Journal of 1856-1857, under March 2.

19. "The Cathedral," l. 658.

20. *Essays in Criticism*, p. 126.

21. *Clarel*, I, 282.

22. *Ibid.*, I, 272-275.

23. *Mixed Essays, Irish Essays, and Others* (New York, 1883), p. 90.

24. See Chas. F. Briggs's letter to Melville, dated May 12, 1854, prefacing "The Two Temples," in *Billy Budd*, p. 173. Mrs. Catherine Gansevoort Lansing's diary, under Sunday, Nov. 11, 1860, says that when she went to Grace Church that day, "the well known, & illustrious Brown gave us seats— he is *very stout*, & exceedingly pompous" (G.-L.C.).

25. See *Mardi*, II, 366-367.

26. *Ibid.*, II, 159.

27. *Ibid.*, II, 323.

28. *Moby-Dick*, II, 232.

29. *Israel Potter*, p. 207.

30. See *Moby-Dick*, I, 143.

31. See *Israel Potter*, pp. 59-60.

32. *The Confidence-Man*, pp. 34, 64.

33. *Ibid.*, pp. 34, 64, and see also *Israel Potter*, p. 109.

34. See *Israel Potter*, p. 109.

35. *The Confidence-Man*, pp. 36, 43, 50-54.

36. *Ibid.*, pp. 169, 2-3. In quoting the five sentences from Corinthians, Melville in three instances made legitimate emendations to suit his purpose.

37. Psalms 28:3.

38. See *Pierre*, p. 143, and *Israel Potter*, pp. 19, 59.

39. *The Confidence-Man*, pp. 322-323. In writing this passage Melville combined passages from Ecclesiasticus 12:16 and 13:11, 6, 4, 5, 13. It is the barber who sends the confidence man to the Apocrypha by quoting the first sentence of the passage given here; see *ibid.*, p. 314. When Mark Winsome refers to the Bible as saying, "Who will pity the charmer that is bitten with a serpent?" (*ibid.*, p. 252) he is quoting Ecclesiasticus 12:13. The confidence man himself seems to be adapting from Ecclesiasticus 19:24-25 when he refers to "the Scripture saying—'There is a subtle man, and the same is deceived'" (*ibid.*, p. 33).

40. *The Confidence-Man*, p. 9.

41. *Ibid.*, p. 17.

42. *Odyssey* (Library of Old Authors; London, 1857-1858), I, 57 (Bk. III, ll. 308-309).

43. *The Confidence-Man*, pp. 250-264.

44. *Diary, Reminiscences, and Correspondence of Henry Crabb Robinson*, ed. Thomas Sadler (Boston, 1869), II, 43.

45. See the journal under April 7, March 7, Jan. 3, Feb. 20.

46. See especially *Clarel*, II, 240.

47. *Essays: First Series* (4th ed.; Boston, 1847), p. 215. Melville obtained this volume in 1862.

48. *Shelley Memorials: From Authentic Sources* . . . , p. 177.

49. See Schopenhauer's *Religion: A Dialogue, and Other Essays* (2d ed.; London, 1890), p. 92; *The Wisdom of Life* . . . (2d ed.; London, 1891), p. 26; and *The World as Will and Idea* (London, 1888-1890), III, 507.

50. *Battle-Pieces*, pp. 185-187.

51. See *Clarel*, II, 135.

52. See *Mardi*, II, 156, 251.

53. *Essays in Criticism*, p. 99. Melville acquired the volume in 1869.

54. See his letter to James Billson, Jan. 22, 1885, [London] *Nation and the Athenaeum*, XXX, 712 (Aug. 13, 1921).

55. *The World as Will and Idea*, III, 414.

56. *Billy Budd*, p. 49.

57. *Clarel*, I, 321.

58. *Ibid.*, II, 285.

59. *Ibid.*, II, 297.

60. He referred to the *Lives* in *Redburn*, p. 85; *White-Jacket*, p. 207; *Poems*, pp. 176, 357.

61. *Poems*, p. 252.

62. *Clarel*, II, 21.

63. Under "From Jerusalem to Dead Sea &c."

64. Under Feb. 2.

65. See *Clarel*, I, 52-53, 254; II, 30, 234, 291.

66. *Ibid.*, II, 298.

67. *Billy Budd*, pp. 100, 81-89.

68. *Ibid.*, p. 92.

69. *Ibid.*, pp. 102-103.

70. *Ibid.*, p. 112.

71. *American Renaissance*, p. 514.

72. See "I and My Chimney," in *Billy Budd*, p. 301, and Merton M. Sealts, "Herman Melville's 'I and My Chimney,'" *American Literature*, XIII, 142-154 (May, 1941).

73. "Daniel Orme," in *Billy Budd*, pp. 117-122.

INDEX

Index references are to the text proper.

Acts, Book of, annotated by Melville, 27; passages in marked by Melville, 38
Adam, 66
Addison, Joseph, 10
Adler, George J., 16, 53
Agassiz, L. J. R., 17
"Agatha" letter to Hawthorne, 28
Ahab, Captain, 5, 57-72, 99, 101
Ahab, King, 61
Albany Academy, 6
Alcott, Amos Bronson, 18
Aleema, 91, 104
Allegory, *see* Symbolism
Allen, Ethan, 13
All Souls' Church, New York City, 7
Alma, name for Christ in *Mardi*, 22
Anderson, Charles R., 34
Angels, 26, 29
Annihilation, 3, 108
Aquinas, Saint Thomas, 13
Aratus, 14, 27; *Phaenomena*, 27
Architecture, ecclesiastical, 52
Aristophanes, 70
Aristotle, 14, 44
Arnold, Matthew, 3, 15, 17, 118; *Culture and Anarchy*, 17; *Essays in Criticism*, 17, 62, 113, 118; *Literature and Dogma*, 15, 17, 40; *Mixed Essays, Irish Essays, and Others*, 17, 114; *New Poems*, 17
Arrian, 14
Articles of War, Melville's attack on, 47
Atheism, 113; Babbalanja on, 24
Athéiste (battleship in *Billy Budd*), 123
Augustine, Saint, 12, 89

Babbalanja, 19, 20, 22, 24, 25, 26, 29, 30, 31, 33, 40, 88, 92-93, 98, 115
Bacon, Francis, 14
Bardianna, 19, 26, 28, 30, 32
Bartow, the Reverend Theodore, 44
Battle-Pieces, 107, 118
Bayle, Pierre, 12, 51, 52, 67; *Dictionary Historical and Critical*, 12, 51-52, 62
Beers, Henry A., quoted, 55
Bellows, Henry W., 7
Berkeley, George, 15
Bible, 61; Melville's acquaintance with, 10-12; Melville commends Polynesian translation of, 35
Bildad, Captain, 17
Billson, James, 17
Billy Budd, 45, 107, 119, 122-123
Blair, Hugh, 10
Blake, William, 117
Bland, 49
Book of English Songs (Mackay), interpolation in commented on by Melville, 11
Brotherhood, human, Melville on, 17, 22, 28, 41-42, 51, 118
Brown, usher at Grace Church, 114
Browne, Sir Thomas, 12, 54
Budd, Billy, 122, 123
Buddhism, 18, 96
Buffon, George Louis Leclerc, Comte de, 17
Bunyan, John, 12
Burnet, Gilbert, 47
Burton, Robert, 12, 67, 87, 90, 93, 96; *The Anatomy of Melancholy*, 12, 67, 86-87